ORGANIZATIONAL BEHAVIOR

DANTES/DSST* Test Study Guide

All rights reserved. This Study Guide, Book and Flashcards are protected under the US Copyright Law. No part of this book or study guide or flashcards may be reproduced, distributed or stored in a retrieval system, or transmitted in any form or by any means, electronic, mechanical, photocopying, recording, or otherwise, without the prior written permission of the publisher Breely Crush Publishing, LLC.

© 2026 Breely Crush Publishing, LLC

DSST is a registered trademark of The Thomson Corporation and its affiliated companies, and does not endorse this book.

971010620143

Copyright ©2003 - 2026, Breely Crush Publishing, LLC.

All rights reserved.

This Study Guide, Book and Flashcards are protected under the US Copyright Law. No part of this publication may be reproduced, distributed or stored in a retrieval system, or transmitted in any form or by any means, electronic, mechanical, photocopying, recording, or otherwise, without the prior written permission of the publisher Breely Crush Publishing, LLC.

Published by Breely Crush Publishing, LLC
10808 River Front Parkway
South Jordan, UT 84095
www.breelycrushpublishing.com

ISBN-10: 1-61433-681-4
ISBN-13: 978-1-61433-681-5

Printed and bound in the United States of America.

**DSST is a registered trademark of The Thomson Corporation and its affiliated companies, and does not endorse this book.*

Table of Contents

Fundamental Concepts 1
History of Organizational Behavior 1
   Hawthorne Effect 1
   Theory X & Y 2
The Science of Organizational Behavior 2
Individual Processes and Characteristics 4
Personality 6
Psychological Approaches 9
Maslow's Hierarchy of Needs 9
Job Satisfaction 10
Job Enrichment vs. Job Enlargement 10
ERG Theory 11
Need For Achievement Theory 12
Herzberg Motivation Theory 14
Five Bases of Power 14
Conditioning 15
Stress 18
Group Dynamics 20
Leadership 21
Chain of Command 21
Contingency Leadership 22
Communication 23
Nonverbal Communication 24
   Communication Terminology 25
Path-Goal Model 25
Vroom-Yetton Model 27
Lifecycle Model 28
Vertical-Dyad Linkages 29
Organizing 29
Organizational Theories 29
Mechanistic vs. Organic Organizations 31
Organizational Structures 31
   Authority 33
Line and Staff Authority 33
Line and Functional Authority 34
   Delegation of Authority 34
   Unity of Command 34
   Centralization and Decentralization 34
Organization Charts 35

Classifications of Organization Structure *36*
Managerial Grid *37*
Classical Organization Theory *38*
Contingency Organizational Design *39*
Organizational Decision Making *39*
Decision Making Model *40*
Implicit Favorite Model *44*
Bounded Rationality Model *44*
Organizational Change *45*
Organization Development *46*
Delphi Technique *46*
Behaviorally Anchored Rating Scales *47*
The Big Five *47*
Total Quality Management (TQM) *48*
Six Sigma *49*
Quality Circle *50*
Sample Test Questions *50*
Test Taking Strategies *93*
Legal Note *93*

Fundamental Concepts

Organizational behavior is the science and study of how people behave and interact in business organizations.

While studying organizational behavior, keep in mind that the attitude taken towards people should be humanistic. This means that each person should be shown as good person who wants to do well within an organization. Each person is unique with a unique history and a unique perspective on a situation. Each person is motivated differently and their behavior is an outcome of their motivations. Because each person is unique, two different people cannot necessarily be motivated the same way by the same thing.

There are two major theories to consider when learning about organizations. Each organization is a social system which has its own set of rules and politics. Organizations and their members usually have mutual interests. It may be a club that enjoys horses or a political party which seeks to better the world. However, in this study guide, we will focus mainly on business organizations to help you pass your DANTES test.

History of Organizational Behavior

Organizational behavior began during the industrial revolution. Factory owners began to see and understand that their workers greatly contributed to the bottom line, spurring on an entire new school of thought to study workers, why they do what they do, how to motivate them, how to improve productivity, etc.

In 1911 Frederick W. Taylor wrote *The Principles of Scientific Management*, which was an early work on how humans contribute to the bottom line in manufacturing. In the 1920s and 1930s the idea was formulated that employees are an organization's biggest asset. In 1957 Douglas McGregor presented the idea that managers make decisions based on their assumptions of human nature. For example, if a manager believes that all people are lazy and will not work unless supervised, that manager would micromanage his employees to achieve what he thought would benefit the company.

HAWTHORNE EFFECT

In 1927 a series of studies began at Western Electric Company in Hawthorne, Illinois. The first study was testing the assumption that the worker output would increase if the level of light in the plant was turned up. To test the theory, they took several female workers into a separate room in the factory and tested their output against a variety of lighting. Surprisingly, output increased regardless of the light level, until it was too dark to see and remained constant. Why? By taking the workers into another room at the plant, they had done something inadvertently; they had made the workers feel special. Experts coin this example to be the Hawthorne effect, which is where an interest in the organization's people's problems effect the output, not the changes themselves.

THEORY X & Y

Theory X is a management approach where you believe that people dislike work and responsibility and are only motivated by money and other financial incentives. It also assumes that these people must be micromanaged and supervised.

Theory Y is the assumption that you believe all people enjoy work, and will control their own performance if you give them the chance. These people will want to do a good job and work better with a hands off approach.

 The Science of Organizational Behavior

Because Organizational Behavior is in fact a science, it is important to remember that theories and studies are created with the scientific method. The scientific method has four steps:

1. Gather information

2. Generate a hypothesis

3. Test the hypothesis

4. Revise the hypothesis and/or draw a conclusion

Experimental research: The experimental method of research is very scientific. This is when a variable and a constant are used to test theories. A **variable** is some changing part of the person that is being studied. Age and gender are variables. A **constant** is the opposite of a variable. A constant is a factor that always stays the same. In an experiment there is an independent variable and a dependent variable.

A **dependent variable** is the variable that the experiment is trying to test or gather information about. An **independent variable** is a variable that the experimenter controls. When an experimenter uses independent and dependent variables, they are exploring the if-then relationship. Here is an example: **If** you eat a pizza a day (independent variable) **then** you will gain weight (dependent variable). The more precise the hypothesis, the more accurately you can measure the link between the two variables.

Clinical research: This is research done with a control group and a treatment group. A good example of this is found when studying a diet pill. A clinical research trial will have two groups of people who all think they are taking this drug to help them lose weight. They are all monitored and report their progress and symptoms to researchers. One group, the control group, is not given the drug. Those persons thinking they are on the drug may still lose weight because of their positive thinking or other thoughts or outside influences. Sometimes a study is called a blind or double blind study. In a blind trial, the patients do not know they are taking the placebo. In a double blind study, neither the patient nor the doctor knows who is taking the real medicine and who is taking the placebo. This helps maintain the highest accuracy.

Correlational research: Correlational research is used to find the amount that one variable changes in relation to another. For example, is there a correlation between IQ results and grades? Correlation can be positive or negative in results.

Some other vocabulary words that you will need to know for the DANTES test are as follows:

Naturalistic observation: observing in an unobtrusive manner.

Survey research: taking a survey or poll via questionnaires or interviews.

Field study: much like naturalistic observation but the observer can ask questions, but does not change anything.

Experiment: an experiment usually takes place in a lab setting, where a researcher manipulates a controlled factor in order to study its effect.

Independent variable: a variable changed by the scientist for the experiment.

Dependent variable: a variable that is changed because of what the scientist has done for the independent variable.

Qualitative data: data that is difficult to measure, or count in statistical terms.

Quantitative data: information that can be expressed in a numerical format.

Longitudinal studies are when the people are followed over a long period of time and checked up on at certain points. These are best used to study the development of certain traits and to track other health issues. For example, 600 infants that were put up for adoption were tracked for several years. Some infants were adopted, some returned to the birth mothers and some were put into foster care. Which group of infants were the most well-adjusted and why?

Individual Processes and Characteristics

Perception is the way that the brain organizes and gives meaning to the information provided by the senses. Perception processes have four characteristics that are:

- **Automatic:** you do not have to think about it. It happens automatically.

- **Selective:** you may be more interested in looking at a cute boy rather than what he is saying.

- **Contextual:** perception is contextual. If you have heard a movie is scary, you may be more inclined to get scared.

- **Creative:** perception fills in areas that we do not have complete information about. For example, when a friend's face is partially blocked by his or her hair, your mind fills in the blanks about how the face looks underneath the hair.

Perception is how we process information, stimulation and organize sensory information. While you are sitting reading this, there are many other senses competing for your attention. You may hear the kids playing, traffic, the phone ringing, smell someone's lunch, feel your hard chair, etc. By choosing to continue reading this study guide, you are using **selective attention**.

Gestalt psychology is an approach that assumes that people organize their perceptions by patterns. It proposes the principle of closure. When someone sees an incomplete form, they fill in the pieces. See below:

Your eyes and mind interpret this to be a triangle, when in fact, it is just a line. This is an example of the principle of closure.

Depth perception is what makes a person able to see objects as they are, in three dimensions. It is what causes some items to look farther away or close up. We see depth by using two kinds of cues. These cues are called binocular cues and monocular cues. Binocular cues are cues made with both eyes. Monocular cues are made by each eye working alone.

The way that we perceive other people is called social perception. Our perceptions are created by three main factors:

1. the other person
2. the situation
3. yourself

There are things that can cloud your judgment when you are trying to accurately perceive people and their motivations. These are called barriers. An example of a barrier is distrust of a new store employee because a store employee stole from you in the past. Another example of a barrier is a stereotype. A stereotype is usually a negative term where you have a preconceived idea about a person because of their membership in a particular group or category.

The halo effect is when one person's positive or negative traits influence their other traits. An example of the halo effect would be that a worker who is always honest with their cash drawer must be a good mother as well because she is "honest" and "honest" people raise good children.

Selective perception is when we limit our perceptions of others. Projection is a term coined by Freud. Projection is where we transfer our thoughts onto others. An example of projection would be an unfaithful husband who constantly accuses his wife of cheating. Self-fulfilling prophesy is when you believe something to be true and because of that premise, your action or inactions cause that to come about.

Julian Rotter originally conceived the idea **locus of control**. Internal locus of control is the feeling or idea that we can personally interact with people and our environment to influence the outcome of events. External locus of control is when a person believes that external causes, such as situational factors, influence the outcome of events. These type of people generally believe in luck, astrology, destiny, etc.

Personality

Personality is what makes each person unique. It includes the way they act, respond and feel. Personality is scientifically measured as five basic traits. These traits are:

1. Emotional stability
2. Extroversion
3. Openness
4. Good nature
5. Preciseness

Each trait spans to its complete opposite. For example, you can be extroverted and be very outgoing or you can be introverted, very shy. Or you can be somewhere in between.

One way that personalities can be classified is as Type A or Type B. Type A personality is characterized by aggressive and perfectionist behavior. A person who is Type A is punctual, competitive, and demanding. They set high standards for themselves and others. Type A personality can be beneficial in the sense that this type of person is very driven and self-motivated. They are on time and like to accomplish tasks. However, there are also negative aspects.

People with Type A personalities hold everyone around them to the high standards that they set for themselves and they do not communicate their feelings well. They feel like pressure is put on them by their environment, when generally it is self-chosen. Because Type A personalities are always rushing themselves and causing themselves anxiety, they are at a higher risk for stress related health problems such as heart attacks. The alternative is Type B personality.

Type B personalities are laid back and casual. They express their feelings well and work through things one problem at a time. Although Type B personalities are relaxed about deadlines and time constraints, they can still be productive. Generally, people with Type B personality have more various interests than Type A people.

Personality is expressed in a number of diverse and complex ways. Personality is often discussed in terms of traits. These are characteristics that a person has which are part of who they are, and how they behave on a long term basis. A person can be funny, outgoing, talkative, curious, studious, and any number of such descriptive words. Over the past hundred years, scientists have grouped all of these elements into five different groups called the "Big Five" personality traits.

The first trait is called extroversion. A person can be either an extrovert or an introvert, or any level in between. Extroverts are outgoing and social. They are often the first person to suggest an activity, and are enthusiastic and assertive.

On the other end, introverts are deliberate and relaxed, often preferring to be alone than with a group. It is important to note that one type of personality trait is not better than another, people just have different preferences. Also, a person doesn't have to be entirely described by one term or the other. Many people are more correctly described as somewhere in between.

The second trait is agreeableness. Agreeable people are trusting, friendly, and helpful. They get along well with others because they are cooperative, altruistic, and good-natured. Generally, agreeable people are well liked and do well in work environments because of their optimistic attitude towards others and life in general. In this sense, agreeableness can be a personal strength.

However, there are also disadvantages in being agreeable because they do not do well in difficult or absolute situations. Disagreeable people are just the opposite. They tend to be cynical, unfriendly, suspicious and hard to work with. While they are less popular than agreeable people, by nature disagreeable people tend to do better in difficult situations and in making hard decisions, than agreeable people.

A third trait is conscientiousness. If a person is conscientious, they are aware of themselves and others. They are responsible, goal-oriented, and determined. Conscientiousness also has to do with how spontaneous and impulsive a person is. Conscientious people tend to think through their decisions and are organized and thoughtful. Neither end of this quality is better than the other. Conscientiousness people are high achievers. They are dependable and persistent. People who are less conscientiousness are spontaneous and interesting.

The fourth trait is neuroticism, or in other words, emotional stability. A person who is neurotic has a tendency to experience negative emotions. For example, a neurotic person is more likely to feel threatened, upset, or angry in situations which most people wouldn't react to. Persistence of such feelings often leads to despair, depression, or loss of the ability to think clearly. The converse of neuroticism is not, as a person might think, experiencing positive emotions. Rather it is emotional stability. People with emotional stability are calm, and even tempered. A person who is emotionally stable feels secure and relaxed.

The final personality trait is openness. A person who is open is creative, unique, and curious. If a person is open they are more willing to experience new things, and are considered more accepting of things that are new or different. Open people also tend to be more aware of their feelings. These types of people tend to have more various interests. Closed people feel uncomfortable in new situations, and prefer the familiar. They dislike ambiguity and complexity. Like the other four traits, both open and closed people have their own benefits. While open people are creative and insightful, closed people struggle with these qualities. However, while closed people do well in structured and specific or repetitive situations, open people are likely to become frustrated or bored.

Often the five traits are scored on a percentile basis. For example, a person in the 60th percentile for agreeableness, is more agreeable than most people, but not by much. A person in the 10th percentile for neuroticism is among the most emotionally stable people. Each personality occurs in many different arrangements and forms, and every person is different. The trick as a leader is learning to recognize the dimensions of people's personalities, and more effectively organize and work with them.

An attitude is a way you respond to a situation. Usually, attitudes are positive or negative. Everyone knows someone who perpetually has a bad attitude. They can be unpleasant to be around and work with or supervise.

There are three parts to an attitude:

1. the thoughts and ideas about a person or thing

2. feelings about a person or thing

3. the behavior and actions toward a person or thing

Attitudes are influenced by four major areas:

1. culture

2. family

3. peers

4. prior life experience

Attitudes are learned and therefore they can be changed with the right circumstances and a desire to change.

Values are also a part of behavior. Values are principles or standards attached to a specific person. Values are generally held by a large group of people in society. An example of a value would be honesty. A belief is different from a value. A belief is something that people believe that may or may not have a fact as their basis.

Psychological Approaches

Biological: This theory is based on biology. People who follow this school of thought believe that behavior and personality are linked to their genetics.

Behavioral: To study and observe behavior. Behaviorists see the individual as a blank slate upon which the impressions of experiences negative and positive can be recorded.

Cognitive: Cognitive theorists examine how the mind is involved in knowing, learning, remembering and thinking. They study how the mind relates to behavior.

Humanistic: Humanists believe that all people are inherently good and are motivated to achieve their full potential.

Psychoanalytical: This theory revolves around the individual's unconscious motivation.

Structuralism: Created by Wilhelm Wundt. The name comes from his investigation of the elements or "structures" of the mind. He emphasized the importance of the classification of the mind's structures and focused on conscious thought.

Functionalism: William James created this theory. He was interested in the "how" part of behavior. He thought our minds are made up of a continuous flow of information about our experiences. He thought that psychology's role is to study the mind and behavior in adapting to the environment.

Maslow's Hierarchy of Needs

Maslow's Hierarchy of Needs consists of the following stages from the top down:

- Self-actualization
- Esteem needs
- Belonging and love
- Safety
- Physical needs

These stages begin at physical needs. First you need to have food, water, and shelter before you can worry about other requirements. Once those needs are met you may start to think of other necessities, such as safety. You might buy a gun or move to a more prosperous and safe area. Once you are fed, clothed and safe you will want to meet needs of belonging and love through relationships. If you feel loved, you may begin to think about your self-esteem and how you feel as a person, what you are contributing. The final stage, self-actualization, you may never meet. Most people do not.

Carl Rogers agreed with Maslow's Hierarchy of Needs and was a true advocate of group therapy. He believed that each person had an idea of a "perfect person" and tried to work towards being like that person as much as possible. He believed that people needed to become "fully functioning" individuals. Rogers and Maslow were both humanistic theorists.

Job Satisfaction

Job satisfaction comes from enjoying your job. There are many components that work together to contribute to that satisfaction. Each person experiences this in a different way, based on their personality. Satisfaction or dissatisfaction comes from many factors including:

- hours
- pay
- benefits
- peers
- social environment
- change of pace
- interest in tasks
- security
- need for achievement

When an employee is happy and likes their job, they are more effective in their tasks. Several problems such as absenteeism (not showing up for work), tardiness, turnover, and retention can be greatly improved if employees are enjoying their work.

Job Enrichment vs. Job Enlargement

The terms job enrichment and job enlargement are two separate elements which relate to job satisfaction. Job enlargement is related to the breadth of a job. Breadth is the horizontal aspect of a job, or how many aspects there are to it, and how various it is. Job enlargement is generally considered to occur in two different ways.

The first is by enlarging, or increasing, the amount of tasks that have to be completed. An editor who previously had to get through ten pages a day now has to do fifteen, or a worker who had to package five boxes of product now has to package eight. This can improve worker efficiency, but it can also become monotonous and tedious for the worker, which is a decrease in overall satisfaction.

The other option is called job rotation. In job rotation, the worker rotates or cycles through a number of different responsibilities. For example, a person may help produce products one week, package them the next, and deliver them the next.

The depth of a job relates to job enrichment. While breadth is related to horizontal elements, depth is related to vertical elements of a job. Depth is increased through factors such as growth, responsibility, and control. Herzberg focused on increasing the depth of a job in order to increase satisfaction.

He believed that by increasing the job enrichment it would move workers from lower levels of satisfaction to higher levels, because challenge and responsibility are aspects of motivational factors. The main problem with increasing job enrichment is that it can become expensive. It can require changes to company structure. Employees in positions with job enrichment, with factors such as responsibility and challenge involved, often expect to be paid more.

ERG Theory

Clayton P. Alderfer developed a theory of motivation that focused on three levels of needs. The theory, called the ERG theory, focuses on the needs of existence, relatedness, and growth. Alderfer specifically related his model to people and their job situations. The existence level focuses on needs related to physical well being. Benefit plans, food, housing, and salary are all considered existence needs. The second level, relatedness, has to do with emotional needs such as feelings of belonging and love, which is equated in the working world as the strength of interpersonal relations, frequency of company activities, and breaks. The highest level, growth, refers to needs such as self-esteem, responsibility, status, and challenge.

For example, an employee who is working a minimum wage job, is barely able to support themselves, and doesn't get benefits has not satisfied the existence level, and doing so is their main priority. An employee who makes enough money to support themselves and gets benefits, but spends all day working in an office alone will have satisfied the existence level, but not the relatedness level, and that is where their focus will be.

Alderfer's model was derived from Maslow's Hierarchy of Needs, and structurally the two theories have many similarities. However, it does have distinct differences as well. In structure, the needs are essentially a shortened version of Maslow's five need system. Alderfer's existence level combines both physiological and safety needs of Maslow's theory. Alderfer's relatedness level is the same as Maslow's love and belonging level, and Alderfer's growth level combines Maslow's esteem and self-actualization levels. The ERG theory is also often considered in a pyramid form, with the higher levels at the top, and the lower levels at the bottom.

The two systems have distinct differences though. While Maslow's method emphasizes a step by step progression, the ERG theory occurs in a progression and regression pattern. According to Alderfer, if a person finds themselves unable to move up in the hierarchy, they will focus on improving themselves at the level they have attained. For example, a person who is lacking at the relatedness level, and is having a hard time improving will place increasing emphasis on their existence needs.

Also, if a person is continually frustrated in their attempts to move up in the company, they will place increasing emphasis on their friendship and social ventures. Additionally, in Maslow's theory a person focuses on only the next level in the progression. A person who has their safety needs met will worry about their psychological needs. In the ERG theory a person can focus on more than one need at a time.

Need For Achievement Theory

David I. McClelland developed a theory of needs based off of experiments using the Thematic Apperception Test (TAT). For the test, people write down what they thought a picture was about. Based on how they answered McClelland identified three different needs. The theory behind his claims is that the people who were shown the picture projected their own needs into it. All of the people were shown the same picture, but their responses embodied three different types of needs. They were achievement, affiliation, and power. His system is called McClelland's n-series, the trichotomy of needs, and the acquired needs theory.

The need for achievement is denoted by nAch. This is the need to be challenged, solve problems, or get ahead. As managers, achievement oriented people tend to focus entirely on accomplishing objectives. While they can create a highly productive work environment, they can also have difficulty delegating effectively, and workers feel pressured to live up to their standards. Achievement oriented people consider others in terms of their capabilities and skills.

The need for affiliation is denoted by nAff. This is the need to have meaningful relationships with others. This type of manager creates a social and group oriented environment. They appreciate their working being complimented as opposed to having it evaluated. For workers who thrive in a social environment, this type of manager would be preferable, however, they can also have difficulty being effective. An overemphasis on interpersonal relationships leads to a lack in productivity. Affiliation oriented managers have a difficult time assigning challenging tasks and monitoring others.

The final need, power, is denoted by nPower. A person who is motivated by power wishes to exercise authority and responsibility over others. This can manifest in two ways, the need for personal power, and the need for institutional power. Personal power is a negative quality in a manager. This type of manager is concerned only in advancing their personal status and being the "boss."

If the need is directed toward institutional power, it is a much better quality for a manager to have. This type of manager is concerned with increasing the power and influence of the organization, or in other words, they are concerned with making the organization successful. They move up in the company through their own capability and are generally liked by others. McClelland believed that these needs developed within a person over time and are based on their life experiences. He encouraged managers to recognize the needs within themselves and others to more successfully organize the workplace effectively.

In summary, he developed four needs for employees in organizations:

1. Affiliation
2. Autonomy
3. Power
4. Achievement

The need for achievement is based on a person's needs or wants to solve problems, meet goals, check off lists, etc. Entrepreneurs have a strong need for achievement.

Based on these theories, a manager needs to create an environment that fits the specific needs of different individuals. Those individuals who are most productive see jobs as a way to grow and achieve.

Achievement-oriented managers are not the best for the organization. They are too task-oriented. Affiliation managers need everyone to like them and therefore avoid conflict. Managers that have a high need to achieve institutional power do the best for the organization and therefore are the best for the company and the best managers.

Herzberg Motivation Theory

Frederick Herzberg developed a theory of motivation called the two factor model. To do this he asked people about times when they had strong positive and strong negative feelings about their jobs. According to Herzberg, there were two different types of factors which influence job satisfaction. They are hygiene factors and motivational factors. Herzberg's theory is unique because he believed that the absence of hygiene factors caused dissatisfaction, but that introducing them wouldn't create satisfaction, only eliminate dissatisfaction.

On the other hand, he believed that the presence of motivational factors caused job satisfaction, whereas their absence, rather than creating dissatisfaction, created neutrality. In other words Herzberg believed that the two factors, and thus satisfaction and dissatisfaction, operate entirely independent of one other.

Hygiene factors are things which relate to the actual environment. This includes cleanliness, benefits, work policies, status, and even salary. On the opposite end, motivational factors include level of responsibility, feelings of accomplishment, recognition, available opportunities, and the work itself.

To put it in context, according to Herzberg, employees become unhappy if the environment is unclean, but a cleaner environment won't make them more satisfied. Also, employees are happy when they are given responsibilities, receive encouragement and feelings of accomplishment, however the absence of these factors won't make them upset.

Five Bases of Power

Power in the workplace is known as a person's ability to influence peers, subordinates and events. Power is earned not necessarily by title but by a person on their own.

Psychologists John French and Bertram Raven surmised that power is dived into five distinct forms or areas:

- Coercive
- Reward
- Legitimate
- Referent
- Expert

Coercive power is when leaders use their power to force employees to do things that they do not want to do. These types of leaders use threats in dealing with others. For example, they may place restrictive or unrealistic deadlines with threat of termination.

Reward power involves using raises, promotions or other incentives to entice the employee to complete their tasks, to be on time, or to perform other actions.

Legitimate power is obtained through a specific position in the organization by a title. This includes the right to fire and hire others.

Referent power can also be called charisma. Leaders that have referent power are looked up to by their subordinates. This type of power is commonly found in the military.

Expert power is when someone is an expert at a certain task or in a certain area. Although that person may not have subordinates, they have power because of their expertise. For example, a web designer may have power if they are the only one in the organization that can provide for a web design need. Another example of expert power is an attorney or doctor who is skilled, has a good reputation, has education credentials/degrees, is licensed, etc. These individuals "carry" their power with them to new organizations or situations because of their background or expertise.

Conditioning

There are two types of conditioning, operant and classical. The first scientific experiment of classical conditioning was done by a Russian scientist named Ivan Pavlov. In Pavlov's famous dog experiment, he would ring a bell and then feed dogs. Initially the dogs would salivate when given food. However, over time, the dogs began to salivate at the sound of the bell. Pavlov termed this phenomenon classical conditioning. Classical conditioning describes a link between a stimulus and a response in which a person, or animal, associates or substitutes a neutral stimulus, such as the bell, with the actual stimulus, the food. Many reflexive reactions, such as a person covering their eyes when something flies in front of their face, or salivating at the smell of their favorite food, can be explained through classical conditioning.

Operant conditioning is a type of conditioning in which a person associates an action with a consequence. The main difference between operant conditioning and classical conditioning is that classical conditioning works more to explain reflexive or unconscious reactions, whereas operant conditioning works to explain elective actions and reactions. For example, a student will wish to do well in school because it brings the consequence of good grades and parental approval. This requires an understanding of consequence. Studies have shown that even infants can be taught certain behaviors using operant conditioning.

Operant conditioning depends upon reinforcers as a method of learning. A reinforcer is anything which makes a behavior more likely to reoccur. Reinforcers can be positive or negative. A positive reinforcer is when something pleasant is used to make a behavior more likely. Parents paying their children for good grades or a person giving their pet a treat for doing a trick are both examples of positive reinforcers.

A **negative reinforcer** is when something unpleasant is removed from a situation. For example, if a student studies more they are less anxious. The anxiety is an unpleasant feeling which is removed as a result of studying, and therefore studying is a form of negative reinforcement.

Conditioning can also come about through punishments, which instead of making a behavior more likely to reoccur, attempt to make it less likely to reoccur. Like reinforcers, punishments can be both positive and negative. A negative punishment involves removing something pleasant. When a child is grounded from television or friends, it is a form a negative punishment. The positive element, the television or friends, is removed to make a bad behavior less likely to occur. In positive punishment, something negative is introduced. For example, if parents give their children extra chores, or spank them, these would be negative punishments. In both cases something which a child would consider unpleasant, work and pain, is introduced to make a bad behavior less likely to occur.

In addition to being positive and negative, reinforcers can also be described as extrinsic or intrinsic. An extrinsic reinforcer is something physical, or from the environment. Anything that originates from outside oneself is extrinsic. Payment for work, a treat for doing well and earning a prize for winning a game are all extrinsic reinforcers. An intrinsic reinforcer, on the other hand, is something which comes from within the individual, or in other words, something emotional. Self-satisfaction and the happiness which comes from praise are both examples of intrinsic reinforcers. The comparative values of extrinsic and intrinsic reinforcers are different for everyone.

The **Premack principle** is a system which uses operant conditioning to make less probable actions more likely to occur by using more probable actions as reinforcers. For example, most children do not like doing laundry, making it the less probable action. However, most children do enjoy watching television, making it the more probable action. If a mother tells her children that they can watch television if they do the laundry, she is using the Premack principle, with the television being the reinforcer.

Regardless of the types of reinforcers that are used, operant conditioning relies on consistent reinforcement. Continuous reinforcement is when reinforcement occurs every time a behavior occurs, such as giving a dog a treat every time they correctly perform a trick. This method creates the strongest associations between response and reward or punishment. However, continuous reinforcement is not always possible. Partial reinforcement relies on schedules. There are four types of reinforcement schedules. They are fixed ratio, variable ratio, fixed interval, and variable interval.

Fixed ratio reinforcement is when the reward always occurs after a set number of trials. For example, if a person wins five dollars every time they push a button twenty times this would be fixed ratio reinforcement. This schedule of reinforcement tends to produce a fast and consistent rate of response, because the person knows exactly what they have to do to receive the reward.

Variable ratio reinforcement is when the reward comes after a specific number of trials which is always changing. Slot machines, for example, operate on a variable ratio schedule. This schedule of reinforcement also tends to produce a high rate of response.

Fixed interval reinforcement is when the reward occurs after a set amount of time has elapsed. For example, if a person knows that they have the chance to get a raise at the end of every year. This schedule of reinforcement tends to produce a high rate of response just before the interval ends, and a low rate of response after it has just occurred. Following with the example, the person will work harder just before the end of the year.

Lastly, variable interval reinforcement is when reinforcement occurs after a specific amount of time which always changes. For example, if a teacher leaves her students alone in a classroom to finish an assignment, but tells them that she will be checking in every now and then. This schedule of reinforcement tends to produce a slow and steady rate of response.

John B Watson argued that if psychology was a true science, then psychologists should only study what they could see and measure. Behaviorism, now also called learning theory, is based on the principle of observing and correcting behavior.

B.F. Skinner was one of the most important learning theorists of our time. Skinner agreed that classical conditioning explains some types of behaviors, but he believed that operant conditioning played a much larger role. **Operant conditioning** teaches that when a certain action is performed, there are consequences. Operant conditioning reinforces good behavior. You can teach your dog to fetch your slippers by teaching him the action and then giving him a reward. It can be said that all social interactions are a result of operant conditioning, i.e., getting peer approval for your new car or earning a paycheck.

Reinforcement is the term for the positive or useful consequence to an action. An intrinsic reinforcer is something that comes from inside the individual, like satisfaction for doing a good job. An **extrinsic reinforcer** is anything outside yourself, in the environment that reinforces your behavior, such as good grades getting you a scholarship or discounts on insurance.

Instructional conditioning gives a negative sanction. Extinction is done best gradually through shaping. Extinction is the process of unassociating the condition with the response. When you ring the bell for your cat to get dinner and then don't provide him with any food, gradually the cat will learn not to come when the bell is sounded.

Response extinction is a method of modifying behavior. It ignores the behavior so you don't have the response.

Egocentric behavior means that a child does not take into consideration other people's needs. This is especially important in divorce when the child is in this stage. The child is incapable of understanding that he or she is not the result of the breakup because for that child, the world revolves around them.

Social learning theory is the extension of the euphemism actions speak louder than words. If your mother drinks, even though she tells you it is bad and you should not do it, you are likely to become a drinker based on her example.

Modeling is observing someone's, our parents' or our peers', behavior and basing our own behavior on it. Bandura also had a theory called Reciprocal Determinism which is the interaction of a person's personality, the environment and the behavior. An example of this theory is that an outgoing person will interact with the environment, say a hotel desk clerk, differently than a shy person. The way they interact determines the outcome, possibly a room upgrade which reinforces their outgoing personality, i.e., if I'm funny and outgoing I get extra privileges. A shy person would not have the same reaction because they would not handle the situation the same way. A shy person would not even attempt to do what an outgoing person would do, hence the reaction is different.

Stress

Stress can be boiled down to the every day pressures that people feel in life. Stress is both psychological and biological. When you get stressed, you heart will race, your awareness intensifies, etc. Stress is part of the body designed to help with survival. Your body perceives a threat and prepares to fight or flee.

In an organization, people with different roles will feel different levels of stress. Air traffic controllers are notorious for feeling high stress, versus what an auto shop mechanic faces. There are many things that can bring or contribute to stress in the workplace including:

- Role conflicts (when two people have overlapping job functions)
- Time constraints & deadlines
- Being overburdened with work
- Not being used to one's full potential
- Inappropriate work
- Responsibility for projects and people
- Meeting goals

In addition there are personal items that contribute to stress:

- Personality
- Divorce
- Death
- Problems at home
- Problems with peers
- Need to achieve
- Poor job fit
- Unhappiness in general

Sometimes, a little job stress can be motivating and invigorating. It gets your blood pumping as you set out to complete the day's tasks. You'll have accomplished something when you're done. But continuous stress, where you never seem to make a dent in your paperwork, can be overwhelming. This type of stress will severely hamper job performance because the worker's time and attention is going towards the stress.

Risks to the individual due to chronic stress are:

- Anxiety
- Fatigue
- Increased weight gain
- High blood pressure
- Drug or alcohol abuse

Risks to the organization result in:

- High turnover (firing or quitting employees)
- Aggression in the workplace ("going postal")

- Absenteeism (not coming to work)
- Low morale

For individuals, you can reduce stress in many different ways including:

- Exercise
- Hobbies
- Quiet time
- Quitting

For organizations, strategies must be implemented to hire a better fit in a candidate and/or match current employees with jobs that fit their experiences and wants. Organizations can also incorporate job training, utilize better communication, job sharing and other ideas that will better satisfy the complex needs of their employees.

Group Dynamics

Groups are a part of every day and every social situation. There are two types of groups: Formal groups and informal groups. Formal groups are groups that are "set" up like a department, work group, study group, etc. Informal groups are groups that are created naturally by people that have the same interests, ideas, friends, workplace, etc. For example, a group of high school friends would be considered an informal group. There are several reasons that people join groups:

- Social interaction
- Need for acceptance
- Self-esteem

When groups are formed, they go through the following phases:

1. Forming (when a group is formed)

2. Storming (getting personality and other conflicts out of the way as each person finds their role in the group)

3. Norming (group becomes a cohesive unit)

4. Conforming (also called performing, when issues between individuals are resolved)

All groups, whether they are formal or informal, have roles. Roles are specific sets of actions, tasks and behavior. For example, a leadership role would be different from a follower role. In society and groups, norm is the word used to describe the status quo, basically a level of behavior. For example, temper tantrums are the norm for two-year-olds. Cohesiveness is how well the group works together; when each person feels and contributes equally, there is the maximum amount of cohesiveness.

Leadership

Leadership is a formal or informal authority figure leading, usually by example, to a common goal or ideal. CEOs, church ministers, and Cub Scout masters can all be leaders. Leaders are persuasive, charismatic, and usually respected. In the business world, it is their job to motivate their subordinates to complete tasks and goals.

- **Trait theories:** theories focused on background and personality.

- **Autocratic leadership:** when the leader keeps the power and makes the decisions alone.

- **Democratic leadership:** when the leader uses group ideas and input to make decisions.

- **Laissez-faire leadership:** when a leader gives the group total freedom to make decisions.

Because of new research, leaders and managers now balance the needs of the workers and the organization. When a manager is part of a chain, it is called the linking pin theory. For example, a regional sales manager is in charge of 10 sales people in his area. He also answers to the Vice President of sales when his group is not meeting quotas, but can send positive information up the "chain of command" as well.

Chain of Command

The chain of command is the hierarchy through which decisions are made, responsibilities lies, and power flows. The chain of command emphasizes the vertical structure of an organization, or in other words the relationships between leader and subordinate. Bureaucratic and mechanical systems have specific and clearly defined chains of command. Organic systems, or situations in which group decisions and teamwork are useful, there is a less strict chain of command. For example, a fast food chain would have a specific chain of command. The employee reports to their manager, the individual manager reports to a regional manager, the regional manager reports to a person above him, and the chain follows up to the owner of the chain.

A school would also have a clearly defined chain of command. A student is under the control of their teachers, the teachers have to report to principals, principals report to district leaders, and district leaders report to the state leaders. Some situations have less defined chains of command. For example, a law firm is just getting started. There is the owner of the firm and a few close employees. The leader is a friend of most of the employees and they often communicate with each other as a group. In this situation, the chain of command still exists, the owner is technically the ultimate authority, but less importance is given to it. However, a large law firm with 150 lawyers working for it at many different levels is much more likely to have a formalized chain of command. Often, the larger an organization is, the more obvious and strict its chain of command.

 Contingency Leadership

The idea that different situations call for different leadership styles is called the contingency theory. According to the contingency theory, while some types of work require an upbeat and positive manager or leader, others are more effective when a strict and regulatory leader is present. This is called contingency leadership, or in other words, it is the theory that a leader's style should suit the situation as well as the task.

One of the first contingency theories was developed by Fred Fiedler. Fiedler believed that a leader's style should change based on the leader's personality and the impending situation. His model addressed three different issues, leader-member relations, task structure, and leader power. He believed that various arrangements of these three factors would require either task motivated leaders or relationship motivated leaders.

Leader-member relations can be good or poor and refer to the extent to which the group accepts the leader. This is also determined using what Fielder called the LPC, or the least preferred coworker. If a leader's least preferred coworker was described positively, it indicated good leader-member relations and a relationship motivated style. If the leader's least preferred coworker was described negatively, it indicated poor leader-member relations and a task motivated style.

Task structure can be described as structured or unstructured. This is the extent to which a task must be done a certain way, or if the task is flexible or requires creativity. For example, an industrial worker must always produce a product in the exact same way, whereas a computer company needs to continually work on new and different products. The industrial worker is structured and the computer company is unstructured.

The final element, leader power, can be either strong or weak and describes the extent to which the leader exercises power over the employees. An example of this power would be the ability to hire, fire, and promote employees. The three elements in various combinations create either high control, moderate control, or low control situations. According to Fiedler, high and low control situations require a task motivated leader. Moderate control situations require a relationship motivated leader.

The contingency theory of leadership says that there is not one single perfect way to lead a group, but that the style of leadership should change based on the situation. Fred Fiedler believes that a leader's style should change based on the leader's personality and the impending situation.

There are three factors that influence the favorableness of a leader:

1. Leader-member relations
2. Task structure
3. Leader position power

When each of these three areas is rated highly, the situation is considered a favorable situation.

Communication

Communication is how two people can communicate with each other. When one person wants to speak to another, they must encode a message to give to the receiver. The receiver then decodes it and can respond. But what do they have to decode, you might ask? John asks Mary if she is having a fun time at the party. She responds "yeah" without looking at him while picking at her sweater. Her "answer" said yes, but John must "decode" the message to understand that she isn't having a fun time at all.

Remember the old game "telephone"? To play, you would sit in a circle or a line and one person would whisper a sentence to the next in line such as "I hate eating packed lunches on the beach with my baby brother" which would be passed down the line, mouth to ear, until it reached the end. The original message was usually so distorted that it made the players laugh with hilarity. This is a great example of gossip but also of corporate distortion. The more layers a message has to go through, CEO to VP to Director to Manager to you, the more possibilities for distortion. A quick reply said without thinking can become "a new department objective" without that ever having been the intention.

When two people communicate with each other it is called two-way communication. One-way communication happens when the receiver gets the message but does not respond. An example of one-way communication is advertisements in magazines or on billboards.

	Low Assertiveness to Others	High Assertiveness to Others
High Responsiveness to Others	Better a listener than a speaker	Good communicators
Low Responsiveness to Others	Guarded & shy	Autocratic personality

Communication networks also have patterns. In a chain, like our telephone scenario, the message is passed from one person to another, sometimes following the chain of command. Another pattern is the "Y" pattern which is where the message can branch off to different departments. A third pattern is a wheel pattern, where a person in the center communicates to the people on the spokes. In an all channel pattern, the communication is not organized. It is all "on" all the time. And last but not least there is the circle pattern, where a message begins with one person and goes around the circle until it reaches the sender.

When someone deliberately tampers with a message, such as in our telephone example or in an organization, it can cause great problems. When someone leaves something out of the message, on purpose or on accident, it is called omission. When you send too much information at one time it is called overload. Overload is when someone can't tell what's important and what's not. Imagine going to the computer one morning and having 500 emails. How can you instantly tell what's important and what's not? When someone doesn't have the authority to send a message, it is refused, very similar to spam received by a consumer. Most is refused, rejected, deleted because the source is not credible, is fraudulent, etc.

Nonverbal Communication

In our decoding example:

John asks Mary if she is having a fun time at the party. She responds "yeah" without looking at him while picking at her sweater. Her "answer" said yes, but John must "decode" the message to understand that she isn't having a fun time at all.

How does John know that she isn't having fun? Because of her nonverbal cues. Nonverbal cues involve the positioning of the hands and feet, posture and eye contact. Think of a child who is trying to tell you he hasn't eaten his Halloween candy but who has chocolate on his face. Does he meet your eye? Does he fidget?

Many nonverbal cues can be taught and used to make you appear more confident in class or a job interview. Professionals use these same tools to deceive and manipulate. Be aware of the nonverbal cues you are using yourself. When you are angry with your teenage daughter, is she crossing her arms? Did you know she is subconsciously "defending" herself by crossing her arms? She probably doesn't even realize she's doing it.

When someone comes from a different culture than you it can be easy to confuse or misinterpret the message. Take into account these famous examples:

- Pepsodent tried to market a toothpaste in Southeast Asia saying it "whitens your teeth" while people in the area chew betel nuts to darken their teeth because they find it attractive.
- Ford launched the "pinto" in Brazil. When sales dropped they wondered why. They found out that Brazilians didn't want to be driving a car whose name translated to be "small male genitals."
- Airline UAL created an article about the actor from Crocodile Dundee, Paul Hogan with the title "Paul Hogan Camps It Up" which in the UK and Australia means "to flaunt homosexuality."

COMMUNICATION TERMINOLOGY

- **Feedback:** Communication from the listener to the speaker which is generally nonverbal.
- **Interference:** Something which impedes the communication of a message.
- **Kinesics:** The study of body language, or how body motions influence and take part in communication.
- **Nonverbal communication:** Communication which occurs not due to verbalization, but through gestures, facial expressions, or posture.

Path-Goal Model

A second contingency theory is called the path-goal model. This model was developed mainly by Robert House, and states that the job of a leader is to use structure, support, and rewards to create a good working environment which encourages accomplishing the organization's goals. The leader should be able to show the workers how accomplishing the company's goals will benefit them. The leader should also provide for task needs, such as supplies and budgets, and psychological support, such as encouragement.

Leaders may choose between four different styles, and the choice should be based on considerations of the worker's opinions and styles, and the work environment. The leadership styles are directive, supportive, participative and achievement-oriented.

In directive leadership, the leader clearly outlines what the workers are to do and accomplish, and how they are to do so. They provide standards, schedules, and instructions. For ambiguous or difficult tasks, this style of leadership can be appreciated and helpful.

Supportive leadership involves an open approach, with considerate and helpful leaders. The leaders create a pleasing work environment and look after the workers. This style is helpful in the situation of a tedious, unpleasant, or stressful job. If a job is repetitive, supportive leadership increases job satisfaction among workers. Participative leadership involves a group oriented structure. The leader asks the worker's opinions and considers their input. This style of leadership is most effective in nonrepetitive tasks. For example, a worker who watches an assembly line all day will appreciate being asked for their opinions much less than a lawyer, who has continually changing goals, or a person feels challenged by their job.

Achievement-oriented leadership involves a pattern of high goal setting and encouragement. This style involves challenging workers, and expressing confidence in their abilities. This style of leadership is most effective in ambiguous and challenging situations, and not for repetitive or simple tasks.

The path-goal theory leaders make it easy for subordinates to meet their goals. They:

- Provide a clear path
- Help remove barriers to the problems
- Increase the rewards along and at the end of the route

Situational leadership focuses on three main points:

1. the amount of leadership direction to subordinates
2. the amount of monetary support for goals
3. the willingness of subordinates to perform

Vroom and Yetton's normative leadership model is used in decision-making.

 Vroom-Yetton Model

A third contingency model is called the Vroom-Yetton model, or Vroom-Yetton normative leadership model. This model follows the belief that every decision that a leader must make requires a different approach, each with a different level of involvement from subordinates, and it therefore follows a decision tree structure.

Using the model, the leader will consider a series of questions that will lead them to styles which incorporate different levels of autocratic, consultative, and group properties. There are two levels of autocratic procedures. The autocratic procedures involve decisions made by the leader, with little or no involvement from subordinates. The first autocratic level, AI, is when the leader makes the decision completely on their own using only the information which is currently available to them, or things which they already know.

For example, a leader must decide how to increase profit, and they decide that they are going to fire one of the employees they don't know with very well. They don't consult anyone, and just make the decision themselves based on the fact that they don't know the person.

The second autocratic level, AII, involves the leader gathering specific information from others, and making the choice by themselves. For example, if the same leader is determining which employee to fire, they may ask a number of employees which person is the worst worker. Often with the AII level, the leader may not even tell the people they ask what the specific problem is.

They still make the choice on their own, and may completely disregard the information they gather, but they do ask. There are also two levels of consultative procedure. In this case, the decision is made by the leader, but there is involvement from the subordinates.

The first level, CI, involves sharing the problem with individual employees and asking their opinions one at a time, never as a group. Then the decision is made. The second level, CII, involves gathering all the employees into a group and allowing discussion. In this way, the leader determines the opinion of the group and receives ideas and suggestions from them. The leader will make the decision based on what they say. The decision still may not agree with what the subordinates say.

There is one level of group involvement, GII. This level involves sharing the problem with the subordinates as a group and allowing them to choose a solution to the problem. When it is important that the subordinates support the decision which is made, or if the subordinates have relevant information to contribute, the autocratic methods are not very useful. However, if the subordinates do not see the problem as important or relevant, and the leader does, the autocratic methods are the most useful. It all depends on the specific situation.

Lifecycle Model

Another contingency model is called the lifecycle model, or the Hersey and Blanchard situational leadership model. The lifecycle model has its main focus on the state of the worker. The worker has high readiness if they are able and very willing to accomplish a task. Conversely, a worker has low readiness if there are incapable, inept, or unwilling to accomplish a task.

By incorporating their task behavior and relationship behavior, or the extent to which the leader is involved in the task and how the leader communicates, it states four different leadership types. If a leader has high task behavior and high relationship behavior, it is called a selling style. This style involves explaining decisions, and persuading workers.

The selling style is best used in the case where workers have moderate readiness. In this style, it is primarily the leader who makes decisions after discussion with the workers. If a leader has high task behavior and low relationship behavior it is called a telling style. This style primarily involves close supervision and extensive instruction. This style is best used when there is a very low level of readiness, such as when workers are unwilling or insecure.

If a leader has low task behavior and high relationship behavior it is called a participating style. This style involves group decisions, in which the leader collaborates and encourages the workers. This style is best used in the case of moderate to high levels of readiness.

The final style is delegating. In a delegating style, the leader has low task behavior and low relationship behavior. The leader will give out assignments to the workers and allow them to function for themselves. This style is best used in the case of high readiness, because it allows the competent and willing workers to accomplish tasks as they wish.

Each of the four styles has a distinct view, however they are all considered contingency models because they accept the premise that there is not a single type of leader, or leadership style, which works best in every situation. They all combine different aspects including work environment, purpose, and leader personality to provide models describing the type of leadership which they believe would best suit the specific situation.

## Vertical-Dyad Linkages

Vertical-dyad linkage is also called leader-member exchange. Vertical refers to the chain of command, the relationship between leaders and subordinates, and a dyad is a group of two people. Therefore, vertical-dyad linkages are relationships between a leader and worker. In layman's terms this could be referred to as favoritism. Simply put, vertical-dyad linkages occur when a leader and a follower have mutual respect, trust and obligation towards each other.

Essentially vertical-dyad linkages are friendships which cause the development of in-groups and out-groups in a working environment. The in-groups receive favorable treatment such as interesting assignments, promotions and raises. The out-groups are the groups which do not share the mutual respect and obligations of a vertical-dyad linkage, and therefore are at a disadvantage. In-group workers tend to be more productive and enthusiastic. On the other hand, when the gap between treatment of in-group and out-groups becomes too large it can become a problem. Out-groups may become resentful or angry, and therefore less productive.

 ## Organizing

Organizing defines organizational roles to be played by individuals, their positions and the authority relationships. Every role should be clearly defined with distinct objectives in mind. The major duties to be performed by individuals, how responsibilities are to be delegated, and with what authority must be included in the organizing process. Organizing should also indicate what resources are available, and what information and tools are necessary to carry out such roles effectively. This is organizing in a nutshell. The relationships in an informal organization never reflect in any organizational chart. There may be sub-assembly groups, stress group or accounts group, i.e., groups of individuals. However, each group identifies itself as a contributing member and acts in unison when the group's ideal or any given member's identity or right is challenged.

 ## Organizational Theories

Many theorists propounded a number of theories of which the following three are important:

1. Classical Organization Theory
2. The Mechanistic Theory
3. The System Theory

The Classical Organizational Theory deals in specializing job assignments, works towards easy managerial functions, seeks to establish authority structures and delegation or responsibility and authority, maintains bureaucracy which speaks of offices and roles, and institutes formal channels of communication among members of different departments in the organization. It deals in division of labor, vertical and horizontal specialization, scalar authority, etc.

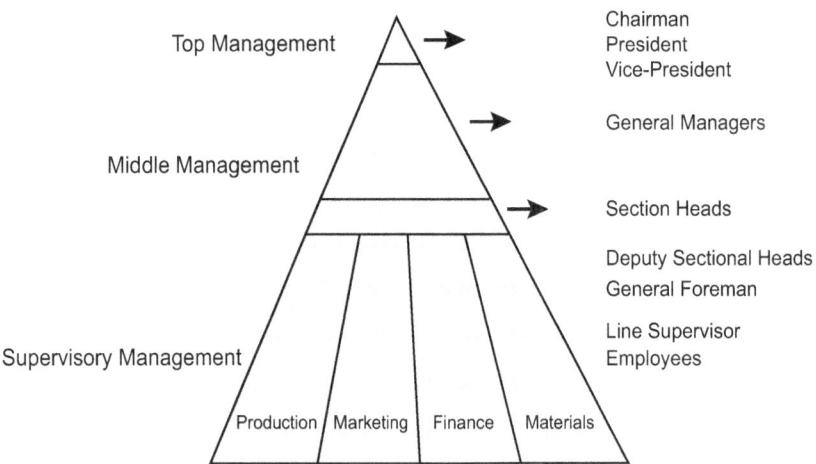

VERTICAL AND HORIZONTAL SPECIALIZATION

The Mechanistic Theory states that organizational change is inevitable and that organizations and people within the organizations have no other choice except to follow natural law. Industrialization brought in its wake a laissez faire philosophy in political circles, which advocated the integrity or virtue of letting the natural process take its own course. This theory was supported by economic philosophy prevalent at that time. In a way it is a precursor to the later day scientific management movement.

The theorists had foreseen the potency of competition. They thought specialization was a tool for obtaining competitive advantage. The later versions of this theory harp on compensation structures. Both the Classical Organizational and the Mechanistic theories took people for granted. This gradually created uncertainties in the minds of workers and opposition started. This situation necessitated bringing the focus back on people. Unions and collective bargaining showed up. Human relation principles were born out of necessity.

The Systems Theory deals with interdependence instead of independence of variables and their interactions. It started with a more intensive, very broad, wide-angle – involving a number of variables to measure complex inter-relationships – and inclusive viewpoint. Group behavior is seen in the system as broadly shaped and influenced. There are various elements in an organizational system but the common choice of an element is the individual in an organization. It identifies the system as changing, evolving and most dynamic. The systems model recognizes the environment of the system and other related variables, which includes all other subsystems and seeks to elucidate an adequate explanation of organizational behavior. The system as a whole is seen as an open system.

Mechanistic vs. Organic Organizations

One way which organizations can be classified is as either mechanistic or organic. In mechanistic organizations the key focus is on structure and inflexibility. Mechanistic organizations are bureaucratic and regulated. There are specific tasks to be accomplished, specialized laborers, and a well defined structure of command or power.

Organic organizations, in contrast to mechanistic organizations, are less strict and more flexible. Mechanistic organizations focus on vertical specialization, whereas organic organizations focus on horizontal specialization. In other words, or instead of emphasizing a chain of power, in organic organizations the power comes from the most qualified person with regards to the problem. People in the organization with higher positions do not necessarily have more power, and decisions are made on a group basis.

Both structures can work well and efficiently in different situations. Mechanistic organizations work best in fields which experience very little change as time goes on, because they do not allow for adaptation. However, many fields do experience changes, making the more adaptable organic structure a better choice. This is especially true in situations where tasks are not specific and well defined. For example, in the technology industry it is important for companies to produce new products that will keep consumers interested. This is not a clearly defined task, and an organic structure would probably be better as it would better allow for open communication, creativity and innovation.

Organizational Structures

Any formal organization can be described as an intentional structure of roles. For the sake of functionality, a formal organizational structure is divided into many departments on the basis of their functions. There may be an Accounts department, a Marketing department, a Production department, a Material department, an Engineering department and so on. A department typically has a Head or Boss followed by a Deputy and then the assisting employees. In such a scenario, the role of the Department Head, the Deputy and the assisting employees should be very clear and the authority relationship should be spelled out. The cooperation of all the people making up a department should be effective in order to achieve the overall organizational objectives. How many people can a department head or his deputy effectively control is the crux of the "Span "of management. There are two types – (1) Narrow Span, and (2) Wide Span.

**Structure
An Organization with a Narrow Span**

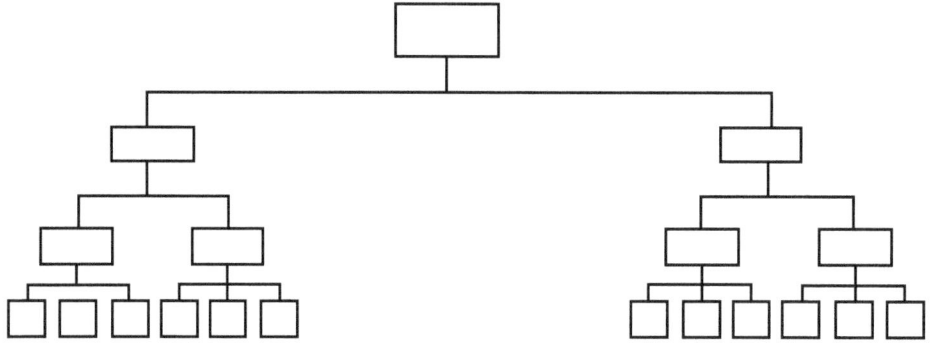

**Structure
An Organization with a Wide Span**

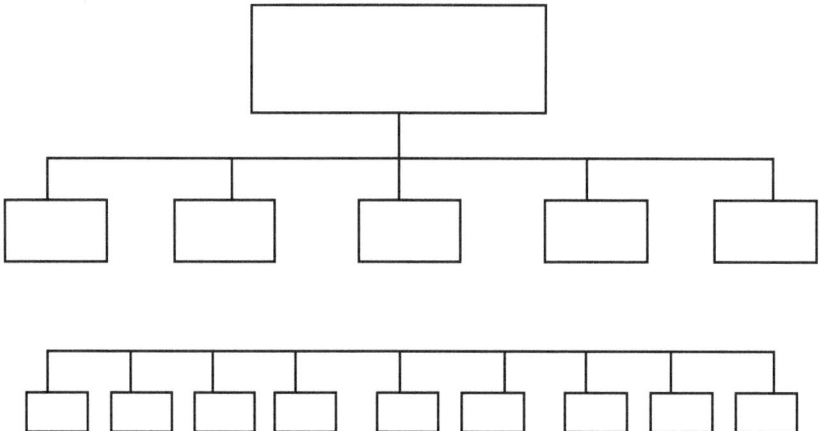

In a narrow span organizational structure, close supervision is possible, while control is good and communication between Department Head and subordinates is quick. The disadvantage is that the super is closely involved in the subordinates' work – delegation is missing. There are many levels of management, necessitating increased cost to the organization.

In a broad span organizational structure, delegation becomes essential. There is a possibility of the superior losing control of subordinates. Managerial effectiveness dictates placing high quality managers within the structure. Delegation of responsibility along with requisite authority is the crux of a broad span organizational structure.

AUTHORITY

In order to achieve company objectives and to sail smoothly on the chosen direction towards that objective, the superiors need authority to enforce compliance of company policies, procedures and rules by subordinates. 'Scalar' authority is identified with rank, position as well as title.

Line and Staff Authority

These are identified with relationships and not departments. In Line Authority a superior is directly responsible for the organizational actions of a subordinate. It entails making decisions and acting upon them. In Staff Authority, a superior is limited to the extent of only giving counsel/advice. The advice given by Staff Authority is not binding on Line Authority.

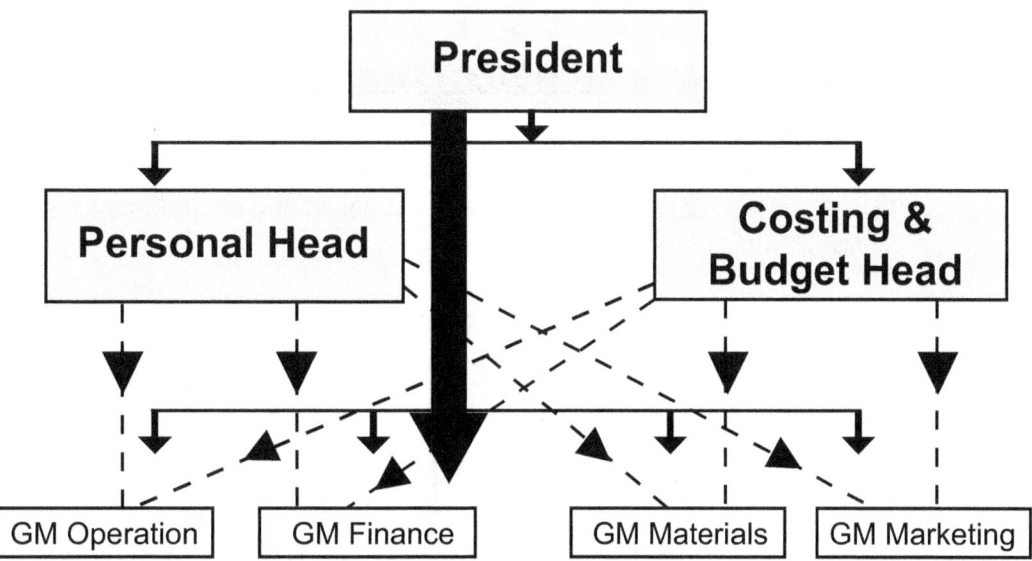

 Line and Functional Authority

Functional Authority is the right of people in other departments (i.e., other than one's own) to control selected policies, practices, procedures, processes or other functional matters with the sole aim of accomplishing set organizational goals.

DELEGATION OF AUTHORITY

The idea behind delegation is to make organizing easy. A collective effort is the key to success in an organization. Delegation of Authority happens when a super-ordinate bestows on a subordinated discretion to make decisions in the best interest of the organization. It can be specific to perform a task or a cluster of tasks, or general, written or unwritten. It is also possible for the super-ordinate to revoke the delegated authority any time.

UNITY OF COMMAND

The reporting relationship of a subordinate will be smooth and effective if it is to a single superior. If an employee has to report to more than one superior then confusion, efficiency, lack of control and total chaos prevails. A subordinate reporting to a single superior is unity of command in its simplest definition.

CENTRALIZATION AND DECENTRALIZATION

In centralization all authority is concentrated at the top. In decentralization, decision-making is widely dispersed. A decentralized authority, if it is re-centralized or, to put it simply, if all the authority dispersed is revoked and centralized again, it is called Re-centralization of authority.

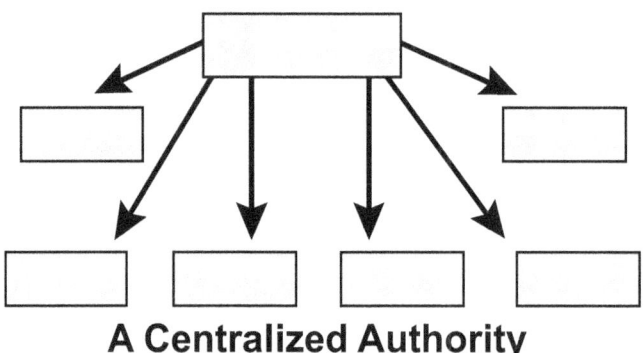

A Centralized Authority

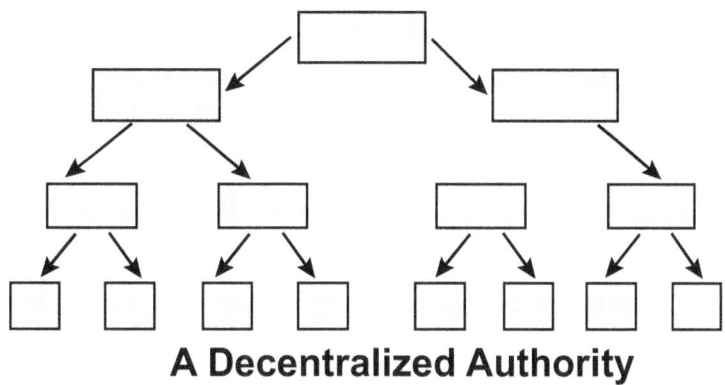

A Decentralized Authority

Organization Charts

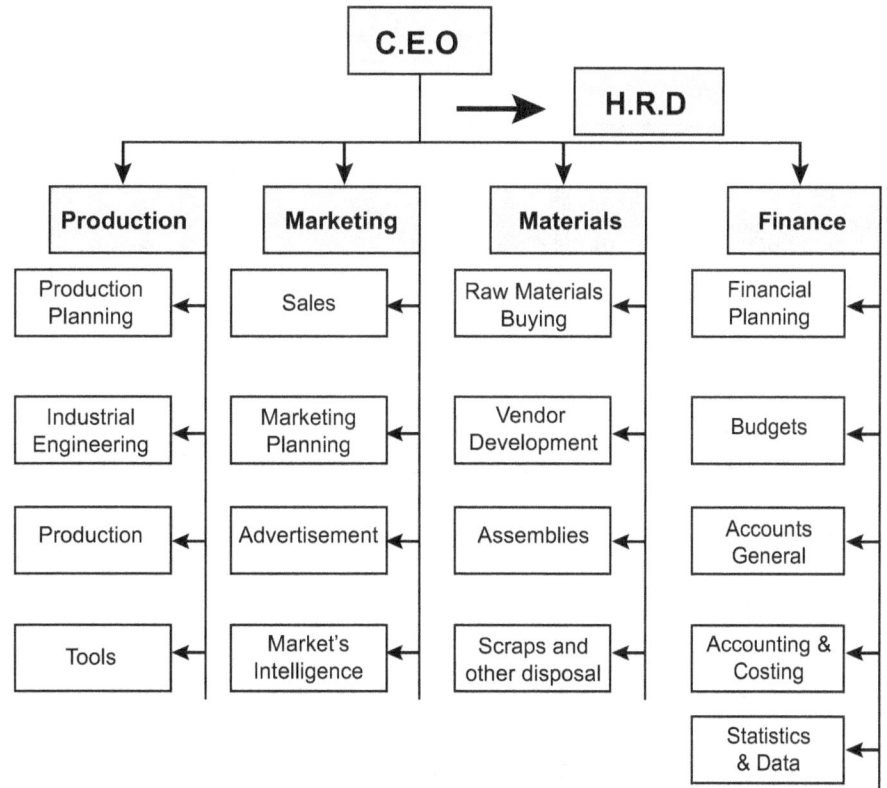

TERRITORIAL GROUPING OF A MANUFACTURING ORGANIZATION

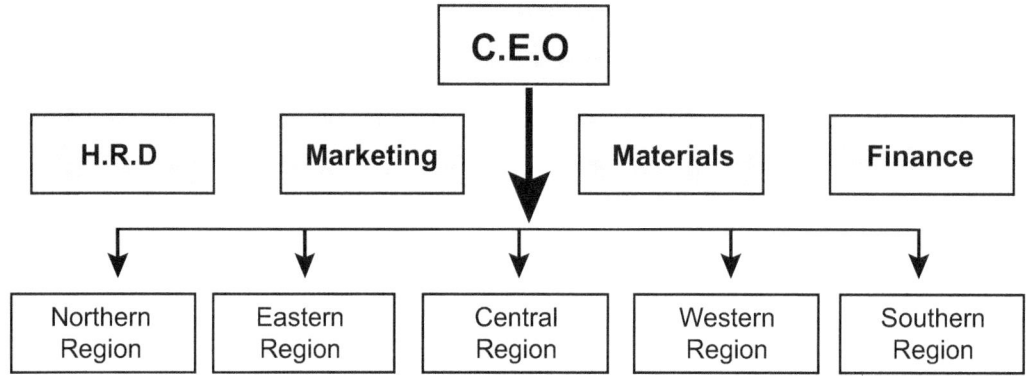

MARKET-ORIENTED GROUPING OF AN ORGANIZATION:

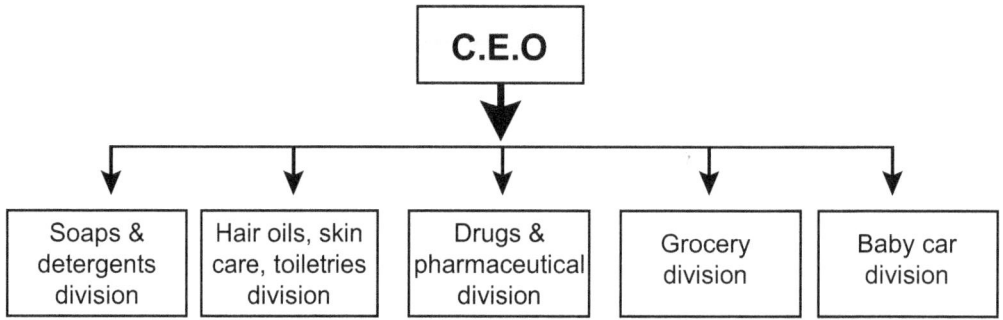

Classifications of Organization Structure

Each group can be understood and classified in the following areas:

- **Specialization:** specialized sections (accounting, sales, etc.)

- **Formalization:** the amount of formalized procedures and rules

- **Span of control:** the number of employees per supervisor

- **Work unit size:** the way the size of the work group affects employee productivity

There are many structures of organizations. The major structures are:

- **Functional:** each group performing a certain task (like accounting) reports to a manager in charge of that function

- **Line and staff:** there are staff departments that support the other departments, usually in charge of producing goods and services

- **Product or divisional:** where organizations are divided by products, with project managers.

- **Matrix:** when departments are structured around a project like a major event or other special project.

Organization structure determines who reports to whom and because of that, it determines who has power. Managers have authority, the power over their subordinates and are responsible for producing results from objectives and projects. Managers can delegate to subordinates to perform certain tasks, but they are still ultimately on the line for performance results.

Managerial Grid

Robert R. Blake and Jane S. Mouton developed a system of classifying managers based on a coordinate grid system which they termed the managerial grid. The grid plots compare production, or how production and efficiency motivated the manager is, against concern for people, or how relationship motivated the manager is. The scale rates from one to nine in each area. For example, a manager who scored a three in production and a nine in relationships would have a score of 3,9. They would place some but little emphasis on achieving goals and place extreme emphasis on social aspects and interpersonal relationships. The ideal score would be 9,9. At this rating, a manager would place equal emphasis on both dimensions and excel in both areas. This would create a productive and happy working environment. Generally, it is inadvisable for a manager to be too focused in either direction, because both elements are important to an effective workplace. The system can also be useful in gathering multiple opinions about a manager's style. If workers rate their managers differently than the manager's rate themselves, it can lead to a change in styles which will make the workplace more efficient and agreeable overall.

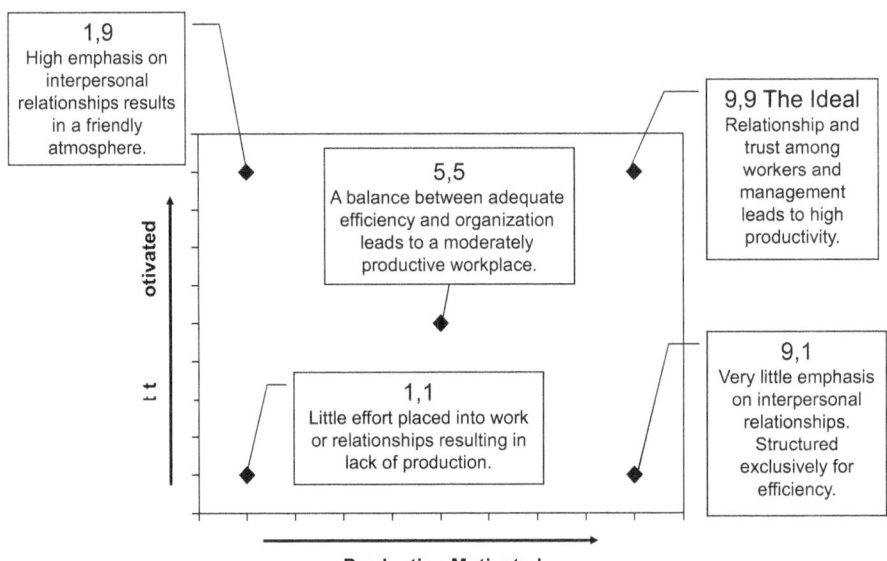

 Classical Organization Theory

Under the classical approach, responsibilities are divided by function, authority level and level of responsibility. Work is delegated from the top of the organization down. This leads to people being highly specialized workers. Highly specialized workers have greater productivity, job satisfaction, etc.

A tall organization is when managers work with few people. This is an example of a tall organization:

CEO
Senior Vice President
Vice President
Directors
Regional Directors
Managers
Sales Managers
Supervisors
Workers

You can see how many levels this is. Many jobs at the higher level will result in mainly meetings, objectives and brainstorming with the "real" work being done at the lowest levels.

In a short organization, there are few levels. For example, a boutique consulting firm may have a president and vice presidents but only a staff of 20. This is a very short or flat organization because there is nowhere to "climb" on the corporate ladder. The leadership in this type of organization is likely to be the founders and it is unlikely that people in those positions will experience ANY turnover. For individuals wishing to "rise" in a flat organization, the only way may be to leave the company.

Contingency Organizational Design

Contingency organizational design simply means changing the organizational design based on the environment and situations that arise. No organizational style is perfect in all instances. When management decides a change is necessary they may have a "reorganization" or re-org for short. This usually means layoffs or "riffs" are not far off as management trims the fat as they combine or eliminate departments.

A mechanistic organization is where control is centralized, the lines of communication vertical, flowing through the chain of command, and roles are clearly defined.

In an organic organization there is a decentralization of control and authority, with the lines of communication horizontal.

 Organizational Decision Making

Decision-making is simply the act of making choices. For example, choosing a new hire or a new supplier by weighing the pros versus the cons of each applicant are examples of decisions. There are three main stages to the decision-making process:

1. Understand the problem and its underlying issues

2. Think of ideas and solutions to the problem

3. Choose which solution makes the most sense

The **bounded rationality** model is another decision-making model. This model is based on the postulation that people will try to find the answer to their problem, but will settle for a less than perfect solution because it involves more work than they bargained for. They find quick solutions to problems by using heuristics (shortcuts).

The **econological model** of decision making is based on the postulation that people will try to choose the solution that has the greatest benefit for them. The problem with this theory is that people involve emotions in their decisions and are not completely rational. The good thing about this theory is that it is very concrete in showing how decisions should be made.

The **implicit favorite** model is the model when people choose a solution immediately. Then they work backward to find the justification for their choice.

Choices that you make rarely, like changing suppliers or deciding a location for another office, are considered nonprogrammed choices, while decisions that you make everyday are considered programmed decisions.

Groups can be helpful when making decisions. They are great at creating objectives and brainstorming. Individuals are better at making the final decision. But when groups have a part of the decision-making process, including the final decision, they are more likely to accept the final decision.

 Decision Making Model

Decision making involves choosing a solution or path of action when presented with a problem or opportunity. There are many theories and models about the decision making process, but generally speaking they incorporate some or all of the following five steps. First, the problem must be acknowledged or identified. Second, the possible solutions must be developed, analyzed, and considered. Third, a solution must be chosen. Fourth, the chosen solution must be implemented. Fifth, the effectiveness of the solution must be considered. It must be determined whether the solution fixed the problem, or if more work is necessary.

For example, if a school principal sees that test scores are down, he recognizes the problem. This is the first step of decision making. After recognizing the problem he begins to consider ways in which it could be solved. This is the second step. He may consider offering incentives to teachers to do better, altering the grading scale, offering incentives to students to work harder, restricting assemblies and school activities, restructuring curriculum at the school, or any number of other possible solutions.

If after consulting the school board he decides that the school needs to restructure there curriculum, he has completed the third step. After having chosen to restructure curriculum, he must follow up, and decide how to do this. He may buy new textbooks, and send teachers to a training conference. This is the fourth step. Finally, in the final step, he will look at the new test scores to see if they have improved and if they have improved enough.

There are two basic types of decisions. The first type of decision is called a programmed decision. Programmed decisions are generally made for recurring or routine problems. They involve using decisions made in the past to solve the problem at hand. If a computer always turns off, and shaking the table turns it back on, then when it turns off a person will likely shake it to try and get it to turn on. This is a programmed decision. The second type of decision is called a nonprogrammed decision. A nonprogrammed decision must be made in new or unique situations. Due to the uniqueness of the problems, the solutions must also be creative and resourceful. For example, a new restaurant opens down the road from an existing restaurant. The existing restaurant must learn how to deal with the competition in creative ways.

Along with different decision types there are different situations in which decisions must be made. There are three basic types of situations in which decisions must be made. The first is called a certain environment. A certain environment allows for complete understanding of the results of a decision.

If a person makes the decision to put money in the bank, they can expect interest. If a person buys insurance, then they know they will have to pay premiums every month. While certain environments are the ideal situation, in reality they are the rarest. The second type of situation is called a risk environment. A risk environment, rather than having all of the information available, is when probabilities can be attached to certain outcomes.

For example, generally when a person gambles they understand that there are risks involved. For each game there are different probabilities of winning or losing, and the person gambling hopes that the result will be in their favor. Another example of a risk environment would be if a person were told that every time they push a button there is a sixty percent chance they will lose money and a forty percent chance they will make money.

The decision to push the button will not yield certain results, but the person does have information about the probable outcomes. Risk environments are fairly common. The third type of decision making environment is an uncertain environment. Uncertain environments require creativity and group effort to be successful. In an uncertain environment, the decision maker does not even have enough information to consider the probable outcomes of decisions.

The two most common decision making models are based off of the different types of environments. Classical decision theory relies on the idea of certain environments. Classical decision theory works on the principle of optimization. The decision maker, understanding the results of their choice, considers all the possible decisions they can make and chooses the one with the ideal, or optimum, result.

As certain environments become increasingly uncommon, so does the application of classical decision theory. However, it is still often used at lower levels of management in large organizations. Behavioral decision theory relies more on risk and uncertain environments, and the idea of bounded rationality. In behavioral decision theory it is recognized that people have their limits in understanding, and accepted that decision makers must do their best with the information they have, or their perceptions of a situation.

Behavioral decision theory relies heavily on the concept of intuition. Intuition involves an understanding of a situation and the possible outcomes. It relies heavily on hunches and perceptions. Conversely, classical decision making attempts to outline the decision making process into step-by-step models for every situation. The type of model which should be used varies by situation. Routine, repetitive and simple jobs can be done most easily using classical decision making techniques. They require little creativity, and knowledge of process is more helpful. However, unique or specialized jobs often follow the behavior decision theory model of creativity and intuition.

For example, a janitor would benefit more from classical decision theory than behavioral decision theory. It is a routine job, which varies little. They would likely create a process for themselves, such as starting on a certain floor or with a certain task. On the other hand, an interior designer would have a different task to work with every time, and would not benefit from classical decision theory. Although there are guidelines they can follow, such as color schemes, they must be able to use their own creativity to do their job properly.

Judgment is another important concept of decision making. A person's judgment, or intelligence, will affect how they make decisions and handle situations. Often people make judgmental mistakes in decision making because of the unconscious, or conscious, use of heuristics, or shortcuts.

The availability heuristic is when a person makes a decision based on a recently occurring event. If a computer company is deciding whether or not they should build a store in an area, and another technology store in the area decides to go out of business, they will likely choose a different area. This is an availability heuristic. Although it can be useful and correct to base one event on a similar event, it is not always the truth, and can come back negatively.

Representativeness heuristic is when a decision is based on stereotypes. A toy store makes bats that are blue because they are primarily trying to appeal to boys, following the stereotype that boys like sports more than girls. Another example is if a company consistently hires people who went to a specific college, because in the past the people that went there tended to be highly qualified. In both cases, decisions are made on stereotypes, and are not necessarily valid. For example, just because people at the college in the past were qualified, doesn't mean that other colleges don't produce more qualified employees now.

A **confirmation trap** occurs when a person is more interested in attempting to prove their solution or claim correct, than in determining if another may be more so, or looking at any opposing evidence. For example, a manager needs to hire a new employee and a person who they know applies for the position. They will likely wish to look at the positive attributes of the person they know, and try to prove that they are the best selection, when in fact another person may be more qualified.

A **hindsight trap** creates feelings of inadequacy by introducing the opinion that a mistake should have been avoided, after it has been made. For example, a company puts forth a product which they think will sell well, and it fails completely. Satisfaction ratings are extremely low and the company loses a lot of money.

The manager and key employees involved in its production feel that they should have predicted that the product would do poorly, and as a result are much more cautious with the next product they develop. The put it through several extensive product tests to be sure that it will do well. They end up waiting so long to introduce it, that another company comes out with a similar product and does extremely well, before the company releases their own. When they do release the product, it is less unique, and doesn't do as well as it could have. The hindsight trap which they fell into hurt their company in the end.

Another issue involved in decision making is choosing what decisions to address. People make thousands of decisions a day, from what activities to participate in, what to wear, what classes they should take in school and what job they should apply for. Leaders and managers have many decisions to make related to their jobs such as which employee they should hire, who should be assigned what tasks, how to increase profits, or any other type of question which is specific to a person's job.

Making quality decisions requires time, and so leaders and managers must decide which problems and decisions are most necessary. They may consider factors such as the urgency, severity, or difficulty of a problem. They may consider what type of problem it is. They may consider if it is a problem which specifically concerns their responsibilities. They may consider if the problem should be made by themselves, or if it should involve other employees.

Authority decisions are made specifically by the manager, based on their own understanding and information which is available to them. Consultative decisions are made by the manager, based on the information they acquire from other sources, such as the employees individually or as a group. Group decisions are made on a basis of either group consensus, or majority rules. A final important aspect of decision making is considering cultural, moral, and ethical implications of any decisions.

 Implicit Favorite Model

The implicit favorite model is a process which can be used in decision making. This model describes a situation in which the decision maker has already chosen what they believe to be the best solution to the problem, or in other words an implicit favorite. In this case, the model becomes more of a method of proving the decision maker right than an actual decision making model.

First, the problem is identified and verified. The decision making must acknowledge the existence of a problem and the need for a solution. From here the process essentially branches off into two directions. The first is the implicit favorite solution. The second is all other possible solutions which have been identified. The decision maker gathers information and evidence which support the implicit favorite, and all of the other decisions are compared to it. If there is sufficient evidence to show that the implicit favorite is the best choice then it is selected.

For example, a department manager is told by the leader of the company that a new employee must be chosen, and he will be the one to interview them all and select the most qualified applicant. He just has to have his decision approved by the company leader after he is selected. Ten people apply for the position, and though all of the applicants have different qualifications, they are all qualified enough for the job. However, the manager is a friend of one of the people applying. This person becomes the department manager's implicit favorite. He shows the leader of the company all of the qualifications which his friend has, and emphasizes his friend's work ethic and agreeable nature. He brushes over the other applicants, and confirms to the company leader that he believes his friend will be the best selection. The company leader accepts his decision and hires the department manager's friend.

 Bounded Rationality Model

The bounded rationality model is another decision-making model. This model is based on the postulation that people will try to find the answer to their problem, but will settle for a less than perfect solution because it involves more work than they bargained for. They find quick solutions to problems by using heuristics (shortcuts).

The model was developed by Herbert Simon. He developed it in response to and as a criticism of the rationality model. Simon believed that there were three steps in problem solving. First the decision maker must decide if there is a legitimate problem. This is called the intelligence stage. It may involve talking with workers, going over budget and profit summaries, monitoring the workplace, or any other sort of action which helps them gather information about the problem.

Second, the decision maker develops a list of possible solutions. This is called the design stage. For example, if a company is not bringing in enough profit, the decision maker may consider raising product price, laying off a number of employees, or cutting production or distribution costs. In the final step the decision maker will satisfice. Simon gave the step this unique name because it involves a combination of satisfying the problem, and sacrificing the best solution for one which is "good enough."

For example, if a mining company receives continual complaints that safety procedures are not being properly met, they may first investigate the claims. They may review the injury reports for the past couple months, hire an inspector to determine what needs to be done, and speak with the employees who have filed the complaints to see what their specific concerns are. Through their efforts, the company may determine that they are not in fact following correct safety procedures. They may learn that the need to install three new air filters, and replace a number of the tools. The company either cannot afford, or does not wish to pay for, the necessary improvements, and instead they decide to install two of the necessary air filters, and not worry about the old tools. They have followed the three steps outlined by Simon.

Organizational Change

Change can be hard for even the most secure individual. We talked a little about layoffs a bit earlier in the text. The main fear behind change is the unknown. People who do not see the end of an action or who have become very comfortable in their roles may fear change the most. Those who are new to the organization have the least to lose as most changes can be very appealing. When people have opposition to making a change it is called resistance. There are different types of resistance. The three types are:

1. logical
2. psychological
3. sociological

There are three main phases to creating a change:

1. Unfreezing – getting rid of old ideas, policies and procedures

2. Changing – putting into practice new processes

3. Refreezing – the new changes are incorporated into the organization's structure and culture

A culture of an organization is the actions, attitudes, feelings and beliefs of the members. It all plays a part of the overall "feeling" of the organization. Culture in an organization includes many "unwritten" rules and expectations.

Organization Development

Organization development is the way that organizations bring about change. So, a better way to talk about organizational development is to call it organizational change. To develop or change an existing structure takes a lot of time and planning. For those very reasons, many organizations put this on the back burner. With any changes, the decisions for organizational development can be made with logical numbers with statistics to back them up, or emotionally, or a combination of both. The human element is very important in all organizational aspects and should not be forgotten.

Delphi Technique

The Delphi technique is a decision making process based on surveys. First, a panel of either well qualified people or decision making people will be surveyed about an issue. Once this has been done, the responses are gathered together, analyzed, and the results are sent out to the panel. Often, these results include the explanations which were given by panel members, which gives them perspective about what the other's are thinking. Also included with the results is a follow up survey, which is completed by the panel members and sent in to be analyzed.

This process continues until a decision can be made. The Delphi technique can be useful when a face to face meeting cannot be arranged between decision makers. Also, if the problem is best solved on an opinion or judgment basis, the Delphi technique allows all the opinions to be shared without the problem of dominant personalities taking charge as would happen in a face to face meeting. It also eliminates the risk of interpersonal disagreements causing disruptions in the proceeding because there is not in-person interaction. The Delphi technique does require time, however, and if there is enough time it allows for problems to be thought out in a rational and logical way because the panel has time to consider their opinions. As computers and the internet have become more accessible, the Delphi method has become more feasible and easy to use.

Behaviorally Anchored Rating Scales

The Behaviorally Anchored Rating Scale, or BARS, is a method which can be used to rate employees. BARS is based on a scale of one to nine and lists specific behaviors for each level. This is useful because it gives an easily understandable numerical rating, but also allows for easy understanding based on the absence or presence of specific behavioral traits. It also considers the employees in terms of specific behaviors which are relevant to a job, instead of in terms of personality traits or characteristics.

For example, a scale might designate a person as a one if they could be expected to ignore a customer and instead socialize with others, and often show up for work late and sloppy. It might specify a five as a person who could be expected to help customers if they ask for it, but not perform duties which are not specifically assigned to them, and it might designate a nine as a person who could be expected to be courteous and helpful to all customers, routinely go through departments to check for cleanliness, and who convinces two customers a day to apply for a company credit card.

The Big Five

The Big Five is the most widely used and accepted model of personality. It refers to five main personality types including agreeableness, conscientiousness, extroversion, neuroticism, and openness. The acronyms OCEAN and CANOE both represent the five personality traits. It is commonly used in the workplace and in creating effective teams. An employer can use the assessment to determine the traits that a potential employee has that are useful to them, that suit the needs of the job, and that work well with the other employees. Teams with similar personality profiles based on the big five tend to work well together.

The personality types are assessed by taking a test with questions that relate to one or more of the Big Five. The test for the personality types typically contains questions such as "I am easily distracted," "I am a private person" or "I enjoy meeting new people" which are answered on a scale ranging from "strongly agree" to "strongly disagree." A person can test high, mid-range, or low in each individual trait. A very high or very low score in a trait represents a strong personality indicator, and a mid-range score represents being neutral or average. For example, a high score in extroversion indicates an outgoing and energetic person, a mid-range score indicates average social inclination, and a low score indicates solitary and reserved person. Each trait similarly ranges from two opposite personality types. Descriptions of the Big Five traits are as follows:

Openness (inventive/curious vs. consistent/cautious)

Openness describes a person who is imaginative, insightful, curious, thinks out-of-the-box, and has a broad range of interests.

Conscientiousness (efficient/organized vs. easy-going/careless)

Conscientiousness describes a person who is thoughtful, goal-oriented, detail-oriented, organized, and self-disciplined.

Extraversion (outgoing/energetic vs. solitary/reserved)

Extraversion describes a person who is sociable, talkative, assertive, emotionally expressive, and energetic.

Agreeableness (friendly/compassionate vs. analytical/detached)

Agreeableness describes a person who is trusting, altruistic, kind, affectionate, compassionate, and cooperative.

Neuroticism (sensitive/nervous vs. secure/confident)

Neuroticism describes a person who is sensitive and easily expresses anxiety, anger, irritability, and sadness.

 Total Quality Management (TQM)

Quality of a product determines its salability. Products enjoying exceptional quality standards demand a premium. There should be a conscious effort to maintain a high quality in not only the end product, but even the methods, systems, communication and thinking of top level to the floor level employee. A good quality program includes:

- Determination of standards of quality
- Institution of an effective continuous on the job checking program with responsibilities and accountability firmly fixed
- A recording system for comparing errors vs. standards
- A method which spells out corrective action, and
- To install a program of analysis and quality improvement whenever found needed.

Checking on the production line while the job is on is a good system. However, it may not be possible to check every piece produced. Here the statistical quality methods come to help. Normally checking is done on a random basis (Random Sampling Method). The most common program liked by organizations is the acceptance sampling method. A sample, normally 10 to 15% of a batch from a running production line, is checked. If they find that a high majority of the checked batch quantities consistently match the set standards for qualitative accuracy, the entire batch (the balance of 90 to 85% as the case may be) is accepted. This is acceptance sampling in essence.

Today there is ISO-9000 (which tells us that a well thought out system will produce predicted quality consistently, with consistency in the implementation of the system at every stage – not only in design or production but in policies and actions of all employees), TQM – Total Quality Management (which tells us to continuously meet agreed customer requirements at the lowest cost, by realizing the potential of employees).

Six Sigma

Six Sigma is a finite, controlled, measured plan that a company adheres to in order to be as perfect as possible, with as little defects, returns, etc., as possible. This six comes from their methodology, no more than six standard deviations from the mean (average) of a statistic to their end result.

What does that really mean? It means that when a product is rated six sigma, the product exhibits no more than 3.4 non conformities (defects) per million opportunities (NPMO) at the part and process levels. The methodology is broken down into two sub-methodologies the DMAIC and DMADV. The Six Sigma DMAIC process stands for define, measure, analyze, improve, and control. This is used to improve existing policies and procedures.

The Six Sigma DMADV stands for define, measure, analyze, design, and verify. This set is used to develop a brand new product or procedure.
All these concepts aim to give a zero-defect product.

The quality movement has acquired many gurus. Chief among them are: (1) Phillip B. Crosby – who always emphasized "zero-defect," (2) Dr W. Edwards Deming – who is considered the forefather of Japanese quality revolution and the thrust of his philosophy has always been planned reduction of variation, and (3) Dr. Joseph Juran who always thought and taught that quality is achievable through people rather than technique.

Quality Circle

A quality circle is a group of volunteers who work in a related area that meet regularly on company time to solve problems and generate improvement in the workplace. The groups are usually small and include a supervisor or chairman. The main objectives during a meeting are to identify problems and to create solutions. Quality Circle groups generally address issues such as safety, product design, and manufacturing processes. Employees who participate in quality circles usually receive training in formal problem-solving methods to apply to specific or general company problems.

Sample Test Questions

1) The way that people communicate with each other using their bodies

   A) Consideration
   B) Body language
   C) Communication
   D) Charisma

The correct answer is B:) Body language.

2) What would a score of 8,1 would indicate on the managerial grid?

   A) A manager who cares more for interpersonal relationships than they do for productivity.
   B) A manager who is highly production motivated and cares little for interpersonal relationships.
   C) A worker who is highly production motivated and cares little for interpersonal relationships.
   D) A worker who cares more for interpersonal relationships than they do for productivity.

The correct answer is B:) A manager who is highly production motivated and cares little for interpersonal relationships.

3) Leadership characteristics that inspire employees is called

   A) Chain of command
   B) Vision
   C) Charisma
   D) Motivation

The correct answer is C:) Charisma.

4) Which of the following does NOT describe Type A personality?

   A) Punctual
   B) Demanding
   C) Self-motivated
   D) One at a time process

The correct answer is D:) One at a time process. Type A people rush themselves and are task oriented, and a one at a time process is much more typical of Type B personalities who pace themselves and work through things slowly.

5) Agreement of members of a group on a decision is called

   A) Consensus
   B) Group think
   C) Meetings
   D) Consideration

The correct answer is A:) Consensus.

6) Which of the following characteristics does NOT describe organic organizations?

   A) Flexible
   B) Vertical specialization
   C) Innovative
   D) Adaptable

The correct answer is B:) Vertical specialization. Organic organizations focus on horizontal specialization.

7) Leaders that use group ideas to make decisions

   A) Autocratic
   B) Laissez-faire
   C) Democratic
   D) Trait

The correct answer is C:) Democratic.

8) Which of the following reinforcement schedules tends to produce a consistent high rate of response?

   A) Fixed ratio
   B) Variable ratio
   C) Variable interval
   D) Both A and B

The correct answer is D:) Both A and B. Fixed ratio and variable ratio both produce a high rate of response. Variable interval produces a slow rate of response, and fixed interval produces a rate of response which alternates between fast and slow.

9) Which is NOT a factor that influences the favorableness of a leader?

   A) Leader-member relations
   B) Task structure
   C) Leader position power
   D) Charisma level

The correct answer is D:) Charisma level.

10) Which contingency theory focuses on the readiness of the employees?

   A) Path-goal model
   B) Life cycle model
   C) Vroom-Yetton model
   D) Fiedler model

The correct answer is B:) Life cycle model.

11) A billboard is an example of

   A) Active listening
   B) Two-way communication
   C) One-way communication
   D) None of the above

The correct answer is C:) One-way communication.

12) According to Herzberg, what are the two factors relating to job satisfaction?

   A) Hygiene and salary
   B) Challenge and motivation
   C) Hygiene and motivation
   D) Salary and challenge

The correct answer is C:) Hygiene and motivation. While salary is a hygiene factor and challenge is a motivation factor, they are just elements within the overall category.

13) Leaders that give the group total freedom

   A) Autocratic
   B) Laissez-faire
   C) Democratic
   D) Trait

The correct answer is B:) Laissez-faire.

14) To "satisfice" involves making a decision which is

   A) Good enough
   B) The worst possible decision
   C) The ideal solution
   D) None of the above

The correct answer is A:) Good enough.

15) Which of the following is NOT a communication pattern?

   A) Chain
   B) Circle
   C) Wheel
   D) Arc

The correct answer is D:) Arc.

16) What does BARS stand for?

   A) Behaviorally Assigned Ranking Scale
   B) Behavior Attitude Ranking Score
   C) Behaviorally Anchored Ranking Scale
   D) Behaviorally Anchored Rating Scale

The correct answer is D:) Behaviorally Anchored Rating Scale.

17) When someone receives too much information and cannot tell what is important from what is not it is called

   A) Overload
   B) Spam
   C) Decoding information
   D) Rejected information

The correct answer is A:) Overload.

18) Narrow span of control is expected when

   A) Tasks are difficult and complex
   B) Tasks require group effort
   C) Workers are poorly trained
   D) All of the above

The correct answer is D:) All of the above. Each of the situations in A, B, and C describe a situation in which a narrow span of control would be expected.

19) When someone deliberately tampers with a message, leaving out information, it is called

   A) Overload
   B) Omitting
   C) Y pattern
   D) Highlighting

The correct answer is B:) Omitting.

20) The Delphi technique relies on

   A) Face to face communication
   B) Guesswork
   C) Surveys
   D) Experiments

The correct answer is C:) Surveys. Using the Delphi technique, surveys are sent to a decision making panel.

21) Which of the following is NOT an organizational theory?

   A) Classical organization
   B) Mechanistic
   C) System
   D) Assembly

The correct answer is D:) Assembly.

22) If a parent grounds a child from the computer after they fail a test, which of the following best describes the type of conditioning?

   A) Positive reinforcing
   B) Negative reinforcing
   C) Positive punishment
   D) Negative punishment

The correct answer is D:) Negative punishment. It is negative because computer privileges were taken away, and a punishment because the point is to make it less likely the child will fail a test again.

23) When information is communicated informally in an organization it is called the

   A) Grapevine
   B) Telephone
   C) Circle
   D) Hub

The correct answer is A:) Grapevine.

24) Herzberg believed that increasing which of the following would increase job satisfaction?

   A) Breadth
   B) Job enlargement
   C) Hygiene
   D) Depth

The correct answer is D:) Depth. Depth is related to job enrichment, which was Herzberg's focus.

25) The organizational structure where a group performing a specialized task reports to a manager in that same area

   A) Functional
   B) Line and staff
   C) Product
   D) Matrix

The correct answer is A:) Functional.

26) Which of the following is NOT a need specified by McClelland?

   A) nAff
   B) nAch
   C) nConf
   D) nPower

The correct answer is C:) nConf. The three needs specified by McClelland are achievement, nAch, affiliation, nAff, and power, nPower.

27) Which type of conditioning reinforces good behavior?

   A) Operant conditioning
   B) Extinction
   C) Classical conditioning
   D) Aversion therapy

The correct answer is A:) Operant conditioning.

28) Vertical-dyad linkages create

   A) In-groups and out-groups
   B) Cool groups and dull groups
   C) Preferred groups and not preferred groups
   D) Popular groups and unpopular groups

The correct answer is A:) In-groups and out-groups. A large disparity in the treatment of the two groups can cause conflict in a working environment.

29) The organizational structure where organizations are structured around a special project or event

   A) Functional
   B) Line and staff
   C) Product
   D) Matrix

The correct answer is D:) Matrix.

30) Behavioral decision theory relies on

   A) Intuition
   B) Process
   C) Certainty
   D) Heuristics

The correct answer is A:) Intuition. Intuition is the ability to see and understand the various elements of a problem, which is important in the perception based decision making style typical of behavioral decision theory.

31) When you are a secretary and there are seven levels between your role and the CEO, your organization is considered to be

   A) Fat
   B) Tall
   C) Flat
   D) Short

The correct answer is B:) Tall.

32) Which has the least formalized chain of command?

   A) A large corporation
   B) A family business
   C) A fast food chain
   D) All of the above have formalized and strict chains of command

The correct answer is B:) A family business. Generally, the larger an organization is the more formalized and strict its chain of command.

33) When the controls of an organization are centralized, the communication between departments will be

   A) Vertical
   B) Horizontal
   C) Directional
   D) Hub and spoke

The correct answer is A:) Vertical.

34) In the Delphi technique, decisions are made by a

   A) Unconcerned and unbiased group
   B) CEO of the company
   C) Random selection of consumers
   D) Decision making panel

The correct answer is D:) Decision making panel. The panel is chosen because they are either experts or important members of the company or group.

35) Which of the following is NOT an aspect of an organic organization?

   A) Decentralized control
   B) Horizontal lines of communication
   C) Loose roles
   D) Incentive programs

The correct answer is D:) Incentive programs.

36) In what way does the ERG theory differ from Maslow's Hierarchy of Needs?

   A) It consolidates Maslow's five steps into three.
   B) It focuses on a progression and regression pattern, while Maslow's theory is main progression.
   C) It claims that a person can focus on more than one level of needs at a time.
   D) All of the above

The correct answer is D:) All of the above. Although the ERG theory was derived from Maslow's hierarchy of needs, it does have distinct differences.

37) When a manager makes a decision then looks for information to justify the decision, it is called

   A) Implicit favorite model
   B) Bounded rationality model
   C) Econological model
   D) None of the above

The correct answer is A:) Implicit favorite model.

38) Which of the following is NOT one of the "Big Five" personality traits?

   A) Conscientiousness
   B) Sociability
   C) Neuroticism
   D) Openness

The correct answer is B:) Sociability. The personality traits are extroversion, agreeableness, neuroticism, openness, and conscientiousness.

39) When you are selecting a new location for a second office, this decision would be considered

   A) Hard
   B) Programmed
   C) Nonprogrammed
   D) Geocentric

The correct answer is C:) Nonprogrammed.

40) Which of the following correctly interprets the two factor model in context?

   A) A person who is very dissatisfied with the cleanliness of their work environment will become much happier with their job if it becomes cleaner.
   B) A person becomes happy with their job when they feel responsibility and accomplishment, but they will not be unhappy without them.
   C) A person who does not receive benefits from there job will feel a lot better about their job once they begin to receive them.
   D) A person who is recognized for their job on a regular basis will become dissatisfied and upset if the praise discontinues.

The correct answer is B:) A person becomes happy with their job when they feel responsibility and accomplishment, but they will not be unhappy without them. According to Herzberg, satisfaction and dissatisfaction are classified by two separate types of factors. One factor cannot change a person from being happy to being unhappy with their job.

41) When you make a routine, everyday decision it is called

   A) Habit
   B) Programmed
   C) Nonprogrammed
   D) Geocentric

The correct answer is B:) Programmed.

42) To carry out the implicit favorite model the decision maker must

   A) Be completely impartial about the options which they must choose between.
   B) Already have an idea of what solution they think is the best.
   C) Be able to delegate research to another person.
   D) None of the above are correct

The correct answer is B:) Already have an idea of what solution they think is the best. This solution is their implicit favorite.

43) When you find the answer to your problem but settle for something else is an example of the

   A) Implicit favorite model
   B) Bounded rationality model
   C) Econological model
   D) None of the above

The correct answer is B:) Bounded rationality model.

44) What is the hierarchy through which power flows?

   A) Maslow's Hierarchy of Needs
   B) Bounded rationality
   C) Chain of command
   D) Vertical-dyad linkages

The correct answer is C:) Chain of command.

45) When you choose the solution that has the greatest benefit for you

   A) Implicit favorite model
   B) Bounded rationality model
   C) Econological model
   D) None of the above

The correct answer is C:) Econological model.

46) Which of the following statements is FALSE?

   A) Type B personalities are generally less efficient than Type A personalities because they are so relaxed.
   B) Type A personalities and Type B personalities are both efficient, they just do things different ways.
   C) Type B personalities are laid back and casual, which makes them unhealthy and increases their risks.
   D) Type A personalities are generally less efficient than Type B personalities because they have so many focuses that they never get any one project finished.

The correct answer is B:) Type A personalities and Type B personalities are both efficient, they just do things different ways.

47) Which of the following are barriers to making decisions?

   A) Statistics
   B) Lack of statistics
   C) Emotions
   D) All of the above

The correct answer is D:) All of the above.

48) What does ERG stand for?

   A) Existentialism Reality Growth
   B) Existence Relatedness Growth
   C) Existence Respect Greatness
   D) Endurance Relatedness Growth

The correct answer is B:) Existence Relatedness Growth. The ERG theory is so named for its three levels.

49) Which of the following is not a type of resistance?

   A) Logical
   B) Psychological
   C) Sociological
   D) Biological

The correct answer is D:) Biological.

50) Vertical dyad linkage is also called

   A) Leader-member exchange
   B) Maslow's Hierarchy of Needs
   C) Vroom and Yetton's normative leadership model
   D) Two factor model

The correct answer is A:) Leader-member exchange. Answers B and D are motivation theories, and answer C is a leadership theory.

51) If you are an authoritarian, you ascribe to

   A) Theory X
   B) Theory Y
   C) Theory XY
   D) Management theory

The correct answer is A:) Theory X.

52) A manager knows that if they invest in a certain stock there is a sixty percent chance that they will make money. What type of decision making environment is this?

   A) Certainty
   B) Uncertain
   C) Risk
   D) Statistical

The correct answer is C:) Risk. Risk environments involve a known probability about the outcome of a decision.

53) The organizational structure where organizations are divided by products or divisions

   A) Functional
   B) Line and staff
   C) Product
   D) Matrix

The correct answer is C:) Product.

54) In situations with very little year to year change, what type of organization is generally most efficient?

   A) Mechanical because it is structured to ensure that specific tasks are accomplished efficiently.
   B) Organic because it is structured to ensure that specific tasks are accomplished efficiently.
   C) Mechanical because it allows for the necessary changes and adaptations for such situations.
   D) Organic because it allows for the necessary changes and adaptations for such situations.

The correct answer is A:) Mechanical because it is structured to ensure that specific tasks are accomplished efficiently.

55) A manager who believes that all people are valuable and want to contribute to their best ability you ascribe to

   A) Theory X
   B) Theory Y
   C) Theory XY
   D) Management theory

The correct answer is B:) Theory Y.

56) If a person scores in the 99th percentile for agreeableness, they are

   A) An extremely kind, trusting, and friendly person.
   B) An extremely creative, curious and spontaneous person.
   C) A very disagreeable, rude, and cynical person.
   D) A very calm, even tempered, and secure person.

The correct answer is A:) An extremely kind, trusting, and friendly person. Answer B describes openness, answer C describes a person who scores low in agreeableness, and answer D describes a person who scores very low in neuroticism.

57) Who believed that managers make decisions based on their assumptions of human nature?

   A) McGregor
   B) Taylor
   C) Ratter
   D) Johnson

The correct answer is A:) McGregor.

58) What is the highest rating on the BARS?

   A) 5
   B) 9
   C) 10
   D) 15

The correct answer is B:) 9.

59) Which of the following is NOT a contributor to an employee's attitude?

   A) Previous jobs
   B) Education
   C) Peers
   D) Family

The correct answer is B:) Education.

60) What is the ideal score on Blake and Mouton's managerial grid?

   A) 1,1
   B) 5,5
   C) 1,9
   D) 9,9

The correct answer is D:) 9,9. This score would indicate a competent leader who creative a productive and comfortable working environment.

61) When an interest in the people's problems affects the outcome, not the changes themselves, it is known as

   A) Hawthorne effect
   B) Taylor effect
   C) Laissez faire effect
   D) Groupthink effect

The correct answer is A:) Hawthorne effect.

62) Job enlargement is related to

   A) Depth
   B) Breadth
   C) Hygiene
   D) None of the above

The correct answer is B:) Breadth. Breadth is the horizontal factors of a job, such as quantity and diversity.

63) When a person acts as expected as part of the a group they are portraying their

   A) Role
   B) Groupthink
   C) Norm
   D) Status rank

The correct answer is A:) Role.

64) Which of the following is NOT a step in the decision making process according to Herbert Simon?

   A) Intelligence
   B) Satisfice
   C) Identify
   D) Design

The correct answer is C:) Identify. Identification of the problem occurs in the intelligence stage.

65) When someone is producing at standard it is called

   A) Role
   B) Role conflict
   C) Norm
   D) Status

The correct answer is C:) Norm.

66) Which of the following is NOT a named for McClelland's theory of needs?

   A) Trichotomy of needs
   B) Acquired needs theory
   C) McClelland's n-series
   D) Thematic Apperception Test

The correct answer is D:) Thematic Apperception Test. McClelland used the Thematic Apperception Test to develop his theory, but it is not the name of his theory.

67) When an employee puts in extra time and effort with the hopes of receiving a large bonus, this employee is being motivated by

   A) Expectancy
   B) Goal setting
   C) Rewards
   D) Benefits

The correct answer is A:) Expectancy.

68) Which of the following is NOT a contingency theory of leadership?

   A) Path-goal model
   B) Life cycle model
   C) Vroom-Yetton model
   D) ERG theory

The correct answer is D:) ERG theory. The ERG is a theory of motivation, not leadership.

69) When your manager completes a job review with you regarding your performance they give you

   A) Feedback
   B) Goals
   C) Equity
   D) Growth

The correct answer is A:) Feedback.

70) Which is the final stage of Maslow's Hierarchy of Needs?

   A) Self-actualization
   B) Esteem needs
   C) Belonging and love
   D) Safety

The correct answer is A:) Self-actualization.

71) Which defense mechanism occurs when someone transfers their thoughts and feelings onto others?

   A) Denial
   B) Suppression
   C) Reaction formation
   D) Projection

The correct answer is D:) Projection.

72) Which is the first stage of Maslow's Hierarchy of Needs?

   A) Self-actualization
   B) Esteem needs
   C) Safety
   D) Physical needs

The correct answer is D:) Physical needs.

73) When communication is given from the CEO to his subordinates it is called

   A) Top down
   B) Bottom up
   C) Hub
   D) Spoke

The correct answer is A:) Top down.

74) Factor that always stays the same

   A) Dependent variable
   B) Independent variable
   C) Constant
   D) Correlation

The correct answer is C:) Constant.

75) Information that is difficult to measure is called

   A) Quantitative
   B) Qualitative
   C) Longitudinal
   D) Dependent

The correct answer is B:) Qualitative.

76) If you believe that all people are good – you ascribe to this school of thought

   A) Biological
   B) Cognitive
   C) Structuralism
   D) Humanistic

The correct answer is D:) Humanistic.

77) Standards or principles

   A) Norms
   B) Values
   C) Rules
   D) Status quo

The correct answer is B:) Values.

78) Which of the following is NOT a factor with job satisfaction?

   A) Hours
   B) Pay
   C) Benefits
   D) Vacation location

The correct answer is D:) Vacation location.

79) When a person responds to a neutral stimulus _____ is being used.

   A) Classical conditioning
   B) Operant conditioning
   C) Extrinsic reinforcer
   D) Intrinsic reinforcer

The correct answer is A:) Classical conditioning.

80) Getting a scholarship because of good grades is an example of

   A) Extrinsic reinforcement
   B) Intrinsic reinforcement
   C) Motivation
   D) ERG theory

The correct answer is A:) Extrinsic reinforcement.

81) Risks to the organization when individuals have chronic stress include all BUT the following

   A) High turnover
   B) Aggression in the workplace
   C) Absenteeism
   D) High morale

The correct answer is D:) High morale.

82) Which of the following is the second step when forming a group?

   A) Storming
   B) Norming
   C) Forming
   D) Conforming

The correct answer is A:) Storming.

83) How well the group works together is called

   A) Dynamics
   B) Cohesiveness
   C) Conforming
   D) Norming

The correct answer is B:) Cohesiveness.

84) Leaders that centralize power and decisions in themselves

   A) Autocratic
   B) Laissez-faire
   C) Democratic
   D) Trait

The correct answer is A:) Autocratic.

85) Which of the following is the Title that protects race?

   A) Title IV
   B) Title V
   C) Title VI
   D) Title VII

The correct answer is D:) Title VII.

86) Which of the following investigates businesses and individuals for enforcement of laws regarding protected classes?

   A) OSHA
   B) EEO
   C) Department of Labor
   D) COBRA

The correct answer is B:) EEO.

87) Which of the following ensures that employees retain access to medical coverage after involuntary termination?

   A) OSHA
   B) EEO
   C) Department of Labor
   D) COBRA

The correct answer is D:) COBRA.

88) Which of the following is NOT a protected Title VII class?

   A) Race
   B) Age
   C) Sexual preference
   D) Religion

The correct answer is C:) Sexual preference.

89) Which of the following is NOT an example of traditional authority?

   A) Supervisor
   B) Vice President
   C) Bishop
   D) Secretary

The correct answer is D:) Secretary.

90) Which of the following is responsible for ensuring employee safety?

   A) OSHA
   B) EEO
   C) Department of Labor
   D) COBRA

The correct answer is A:) OSHA.

91) Which of the following is NOT a way to deal with risk?

   A) Assuming
   B) Avoiding
   C) Shifting
   D) Deflecting

The correct answer is D:) Deflecting.

92) Which of the following is an example of environmental stress?

   A) Construction noise
   B) Strong perfume
   C) Peers
   D) Broken heating unit

The correct answer is A:) Construction noise.

93) Which of the following is an example of Maslow's first level of needs?

   A) Food
   B) Car
   C) School
   D) Church

The correct answer is A:) Food.

94) Which is the second stage of Maslow's Hierarchy of Needs?

   A) Self-actualization
   B) Esteem needs
   C) Safety needs
   D) Physical needs

The correct answer is C:) Safety needs.

95) When you choose the best action for each situation

   A) Situational leadership
   B) Participative leadership
   C) Autocratic leadership
   D) Laissez faire leadership

The correct answer is A:) Situational leadership.

96) When a supervisor asks for opinions in making decisions

   A) Situational leadership
   B) Participative leadership
   C) Autocratic leadership
   D) Laissez faire leadership

The correct answer is B:) Participative leadership.

97) Which of the following is a union function?

　　A) Negotiate pay
　　B) Creating new business policies
　　C) Budgeting
　　D) Creating statistical reports

The correct answer is A:) Negotiate pay.

98) Which of the following is an example of Maslow's third level of needs?

　　A) Sex
　　B) Money
　　C) Love
　　D) Home

The correct answer is C:) Love.

99) Which of the following is NOT part of a training program?

　　A) Job sharing
　　B) Job rotating
　　C) Temporary promotion
　　D) Promotion

The correct answer is D:) Promotion.

100) A doctor who is skilled, has a good reputation, has education credentials/degrees, is licensed has _____ power.

　　A) Coercive
　　B) Referent
　　C) Legitimate
　　D) Expert

The correct answer is D:) Expert.

101) Hands off leadership

   A) Situational leadership
   B) Participative leadership
   C) Autocratic leadership
   D) Laissez faire leadership

The correct answer is D:) Laissez faire leadership.

102) Which of the following tells employees and others what is the main purpose of the company is

   A) Vision
   B) Mission statement
   C) Company statement
   D) Business plan

The correct answer is B:) Mission statement.

103) A policy can be defined as a _____ action course that serves as a guide for the identified and accepted objectives and goals.

   A) Predefined
   B) Flexible
   C) Necessary
   D) Unknown

The correct answer is A:) Predefined.

104) A totalitarian leader

   A) Situational leadership
   B) Participative leadership
   C) Sutocratic leadership
   D) Laissez faire leadership

The correct answer is C:) Sutocratic leadership.

105) Which of the following is NOT a supervisory function?

   A) Marketing
   B) Planning
   C) Staffing
   D) Organizing

The correct answer is A:) Marketing.

106) The Delphi method consists of

   A) Surveys
   B) Interviews
   C) Questionnaires
   D) None of the above

The correct answer is C:) Questionnaires. A facilitator sends out questionnaires which pertain to a particular topic, and a group of participants anonymously respond to the questionnaires.

107) Which of the following is an example of an extrinsic reward?

   A) Raise
   B) Self-esteem
   C) Praise
   D) Personal development

The correct answer is A:) Raise.

108) If a plant manager is tasked to reduce costs by 10% this is an example of what kind of goal?

   A) Strategic
   B) Long-term
   C) Tactical
   D) Operational

The correct answer is D:) Operational.

109) Which of the following shows the relationship between employees and their peers?

   A) Organizational chart
   B) Gantt chart
   C) Decision tree
   D) Simulation

The correct answer is A:) Organizational chart.

110) Which of the following shows alternate paths for decision making?

   A) Organizational chart
   B) Gantt chart
   C) Decision tree
   D) Simulation

The correct answer is C:) Decision tree.

111) When a supervisor administers a questionnaire among participants that have never met it is called

   A) Brainstorming
   B) Sampling
   C) Delphi technique
   D) Groupthink

The correct answer is C:) Delphi technique.

112) Which of the following shows a timeline for projects?

   A) Organizational chart
   B) Gantt chart
   C) Decision tree
   D) Simulation

The correct answer is B:) Gantt chart.

113) Who created Theory X and Theory Y?

   A) Max Weber
   B) Abraham Maslow
   C) Douglas McGregor
   D) Frank Gilbreth

The correct answer is C:) Douglas McGregor.

114) Members of a quality circle

I. Are volunteers
II. Meet on company time
III. Are paid according to their contributions

   A) I and II
   B) II and III
   C) I and III
   D) I, II, and III

The correct answer is A:) I and II.

115) Agreeableness is one of the big five personality types. Which of the following is NOT a characteristic of agreeableness?

   A) Friendly
   B) Sensitive
   C) Compassionate
   D) None of the above

The correct answer is B:) Sensitive. Agreeableness describes a person who is trusting, altruistic, kind, affectionate, compassionate, and cooperative. Sensitivity is a characteristic of neuroticism.

116) When two groups or individuals work together to resolve a problem it is called

   A) Negotiation
   B) Grievance
   C) Arbitration
   D) Mediation

The correct answer is A:) Negotiation.

117) Power is obtained through a specific position in the organization by a title

   A) Coercive power
   B) Referent power
   C) Legitimate power
   D) Expert power

The correct answer is C:) Legitimate power.

118) An employee that works on an assembly line performing the same task again and again is an example of

   A) Job specialization
   B) Job rotation
   C) Job sharing
   D) None of the above

The correct answer is A:) Job specialization.

119) Two receptionists work at Widget, Inc., one in the morning and one in the afternoon. They are an example of

   A) Job specialization
   B) Job rotation
   C) Job sharing
   D) None of the above

The correct answer is C:) Job sharing.

120) When a person acts as expected as part of the group they are portraying their

   A) Role
   B) Groupthink
   C) Norm
   D) Status rank

The correct answer is A:) Role.

121) Social security benefits are based on the primary insurance amount, which is formulated using average wage indices and bend points. A COLA increases which of the following?

A) Bend points
B) Average wage indices
C) Primary insurance amount
D) None of the above

The correct answer is C:) Primary insurance amount. A COLA affects social security benefits.

122) Which of the following is an example of a compressed work week schedule?

A) Four 8 hour shifts
B) Four 10 hour shifts
C) Five 8 hour shifts
D) Five 10 hour shifts

The correct answer is B:) Four 10 hour shifts. A compressed work week schedule allows an employee works the same amount of hours weekly in less workdays.

123) Dual career ladder programs are most common in what industry?

A) Engineering
B) Scientific
C) Medical
D) All of the above

The correct answer is D:) All of the above. All of the above careers offer jobs that provide higher pay for more expertise in the field.

124) Who first studied job motions with bricklayers, studying how fewer hand motions made the work faster?

A) Max Weber
B) Abraham Maslow
C) Douglas McGregor
D) Frank Gilbreth

The correct answer is D:) Frank Gilbreth.

125) When someone is producing at standard it is called

   A) Role
   B) Role conflict
   C) Norm
   D) Status

The correct answer is C:) Norm.

126) What is it called when a third party of empowered to resolve a disagreement it is called?

   A) Negotiation
   B) Grievance
   C) Arbitration
   D) Mediation

The correct answer is C:) Arbitration.

127) Who was a proponent of bureaucracy?

   A) Max Weber
   B) Abraham Maslow
   C) Douglas McGregor
   D) Frank Gilbreth

The correct answer is A:) Max Weber.

128) What is a formal complaint called?

   A) Negotiation
   B) Grievance
   C) Arbitration
   D) Mediation

The correct answer is B:) Grievance.

129) The science of body language is called

   A) Dialect
   B) Pronunciation
   C) Kinesics
   D) Monotone

The correct answer is C:) Kinesics. Kinesics is the study of body language in respect to communication.

130) Which of the following is the theory of autonomy that depends on a corporation's approach to globalization?

   A) Limited autonomy
   B) Variable autonomy
   C) Negotiable autonomy
   D) Dependant autonomy

The correct answer is A:) Limited autonomy. There are three theories concerning subsidiary's autonomy in decision-making.

131) What is the main goal of a quality circle?

   A) To meet the goals of manufacturing processes efficiently
   B) To review the quality of products and identify product design flaws
   C) To solve problems and generate improvement in the workplace
   D) All of the above

The correct answer is C:) To solve problems and generate improvement in the workplace. Quality circles are designed to identify problems and to create solutions.

132) This power is also known as charisma

   A) Coercive power
   B) Referent power
   C) Reward power
   D) Expert power

The correct answer is B:) Referent power.

133) To motivate line employees and keep them interested in their work, supervisors may institute any of the following BUT

   A) Job specialization
   B) Job rotation
   C) Mentoring
   D) Four day work weeks

The correct answer is A:) Job specialization.

134) The grapevine of the organization is everything BUT

   A) Formal
   B) Generally accurate
   C) Verbal
   D) Exists in every organization

The correct answer is A:) Formal.

135) When a supervisor believes that all employees like work it is called

   A) Theory Y
   B) Theory X
   C) Hawthorne Effect
   D) TQM

The correct answer is A:) Theory Y.

136) This scientific study originally tested worker's output and light, later revealing unintended consequences

   A) Theory Y
   B) Theory X
   C) Hawthorne Effect
   D) TQM

The correct answer is C:) Hawthorne Effect.

137) The Equal Pay Act protects against pay discrimination based on _____ for employees who perform the same work.

A) Age
B) Gender
C) Race
D) All of the above

The correct answer is B:) Gender.

138) An accountant says he is having back pain. He asks his employer for an ergonomic chair. The employee has no obvious disability or known medical condition. His employer asks him to provide documentation from a physician that describes his disability and substantiates his need for an ergonomic chair. According to ergonomics and reasonable accommodation:

A) The employer is not required to provide a new chair because only giving Paul a new chair is favoritism.
B) Because no other accountant has need for an ergonomic chair, it does not fall under the category of reasonable accommodation.
C) The employer is required to provide a new chair with or without the documentation.
D) The employer is only required to provide a new chair with the documentation.

The correct answer is D:) The employer is only required to provide a new chair with the documentation. Because the disability and need for accommodation is not obvious, the employee must provide the documentation or the employer can refuse to provide the chair.

139) Referent power is the same as

A) Lassaize faire leadership
B) Charismatic leadership
C) Peer pressure
D) Expert leadership

The correct answer is B:) Charismatic leadership.

140) Legitimate power is the same as

   A) Lassaize faire leadership
   B) Traditional leadership
   C) Peer pressure
   D) Expert leadership

The correct answer is B:) Traditional leadership.

141) Regarding sexual harassment which of the following is NOT true

   A) Offenders can be same or opposite sex
   B) Victims do not have to be harassed personally but affected through environment
   C) Harasser must be a superior employee
   D) Harassment may occur without economic injury

The correct answer is C:) Harasser must be a superior employee.

142) When leaders use their power to force employees to do things that they do not want to do this is called

   A) Coercive power
   B) Referent power
   C) Reward power
   D) Expert power

The correct answer is A:) Coercive power.

143) Long term success through customer satisfaction

   A) Theory Y
   B) Theory X
   C) Hawthorne Effect
   D) TQM

The correct answer is D:) TQM.

144) Quality circles address problems such as

   A) Safety
   B) Product design
   C) Manufacturing processes
   D) All of the above

The correct answer is D:) All of the above. Quality circles address problems such as safety, product design, and manufacturing processes.

145) Which of the following correctly shows the personality types represented by the acronym OCEAN?

   A) Affectionate, conscientiousness, extroversion, neuroticism, and openness
   B) Extroversion, neuroticism, friendliness, openness, and kindness
   C) Conscientiousness, extroversion, agreeableness, neuroticism, and openness
   D) Openness, niceness, conscientiousness, extroversion, and agreeableness

The correct answer is C:) Conscientiousness, extroversion, agreeableness, neuroticism, and openness. OCEAN refers to the Big Five personality types.

146) Who was responsible for developing the 14 principles of management?

   A) Max Weber
   B) Henri Fayol
   C) Douglas McGregor
   D) Frank Gilbreth

The correct answer is B:) Henri Fayol.

147) The Delphi technique is designed to

   A) Solve problems through group discussion
   B) Create a majority group opinion on a particular topic
   C) Identify key agreements and disagreements on a real-world topic
   D) Analyze all aspects of a situation from multiple points of view

The correct answer is B:) Create a majority group opinion on a particular topic.

148) Herzberg believed that increasing which of the following would increase job satisfaction?

   A) Breadth
   B) Job enlargement
   C) Hygiene
   D) Depth

The correct answer is D:) Depth. Depth is related to job enrichment, which was Herzberg's focus.

149) Fast food places do not pay their workers less than minimum wage because it is against the law. Which of Kohlberg's stages does this describe?

   A) Stage 1
   B) Stage 2
   C) Stage 3
   D) Stage 4

The correct answer is D:) Stage 4. In Stage 4, people are motivated primarily by authority, such as the law.

150) Which of the following is NOT an example of nonverbal communication?

   A) Crossing your arms
   B) Posture
   C) Eye contact
   D) Whispering

The correct answer is D:) Whispering.

151) Which of the following industries is part of a dynamic environment, meaning the market is constantly changing and updating?

   A) Nurseries
   B) Education
   C) Electronics
   D) Manufacturing

The correct answer is C:) Electronics.

152) When a person believes their culture is superior to all other cultures it is called

   A) Ethnocentrism
   B) Interference
   C) Situation
   D) Plagiarism

The correct answer is A:) Ethnocentrism.

153) Which of the following became famous for his experiments with dogs and conditioning?

   A) Alfred Kinsey
   B) Carl Jung
   C) B. F. Skinner
   D) Ivan Pavlov

The correct answer is D:) Ivan Pavlov.

154) The organizational structure where there are staff departments that support other departments

   A) Functional
   B) Line and staff
   C) Product
   D) Matrix

The correct answer is B:) Line and staff.

155) What type of research is conducted by watching the subject?

   A) Naturalistic observation
   B) Longitudinal research
   C) Conditioning
   D) Operant conditioning

The correct answer is A:) Naturalistic observation.

156) The Delphi process takes place in what length of time?

   A) The Delphi method is usually a long process that continues as long as necessary to form a consensus.
   B) The Delphi method is usually a long process that continues until the participants reach the correct answer.
   C) The Delphi method is usually a short process that takes no longer than a week.
   D) The Delphi method is usually a short process that takes place in a single day.

The correct answer is A:) The Delphi method is usually a long process that continues as long as necessary to form a consensus.

157) Who created a system of human needs and motivations?

   A) Max Weber
   B) Abraham Maslow
   C) Douglas McGregor
   D) Frank Gilbreth

The correct answer is B:) Abraham Maslow.

158) What is it called when a third party is facilitating negotiations?

   A) Concession
   B) Grievance
   C) Arbitration
   D) Mediation

The correct answer is D:) Mediation.

159) Which of the following is an industry commonly known to have line employees?

   A) Automotive
   B) Woodworking
   C) Education
   D) Retail

The correct answer is A:) Automotive.

160) The value in the Delphi technique lies in the _____ it creates.

A) Information
B) Conversation
C) Thinking
D) Ideas

The correct answer is D:) Ideas. Though the goal is to obtain a single expert opinion, the new ideas and differing opinions that often form are also valuable.

161) The Big Five personality types are assessed through a test. People with similar scores

A) Tend to work well together
B) Should not work together
C) Do not balance each other out
D) Two of the above

The correct answer is A:) Tend to work well together. People with similar scores usually have similar work attitudes, similar problem solving methods, and respond well to each other's demeanor.

162) In a compressed work week schedule, an employee works a usual 35-40 hour workweek in less than ___ days.

A) 4
B) 5
C) 6
D) 7

The correct answer is B:) 5.

163) Dual career ladder programs are designed for employees who

A) Have technical skills and also want to work in a managerial capacity
B) Have managerial skills and also want to work in a technical capacity
C) Have technical skills and do not want to work in a managerial capacity
D) Have managerial skills and do not want to work in a technical capacity

The correct answer is C:) Have technical skills and do not want to work in a managerial capacity.

164) Which of the following is NOT one of the five bases of power?

   A) Coercive
   B) Enterprising
   C) Legitimate
   D) Expert

The correct answer is B:) Enterprising. The five bases of power are coercive, reward, legitimate, referent, and expert.

165) Which of the following is NOT part of the perceptual model of communication?

   A) Message
   B) Sender
   C) Recipient
   D) Noise

The correct answer is D:) Noise.

166) When decisions are made by top management it is referred to as

   A) Centralized decision making
   B) Organizational decision making
   C) Change
   D) Organizational decline

The correct answer is A:) Centralized decision making.

167) Female leaders use which type of leadership more than male leaders?

   A) Path-goal
   B) Transactional
   C) Transformational
   D) Servant

The correct answer is C:) Transformational.

Test Taking Strategies

Here are some test-taking strategies that are specific to this test and to other DSST tests in general:

- Keep your eyes on the time. Pay attention to how much time you have left.
- Read the entire question and read all the answers. Many questions are not as hard to answer as they may seem. Sometimes, a difficult sounding question really only is asking you how to read an accompanying chart. Chart and graph questions are on most DANTES/DSST tests and should be an easy free point.
- If you don't know the answer immediately, the new computer-based testing lets you mark questions and come back to them later if you have time.
- Read the wording carefully. Some words can give you hints to the right answer. There are no exceptions to an answer when there are words in the question such as always, all or none. If one of the answer choices includes most or some of the right answers, but not all, then that is not the answer. Here is an example:

> The primary colors include all of the following:
>
> A) Red, Yellow, Blue, Green
>
> B) Red, Green, Yellow
>
> C) Red, Orange, Yellow
>
> D) Red, Yellow, Blue

Although item A includes all the right answers, it also includes an incorrect answer, making it incorrect. If you didn't read it carefully, were in a hurry, or didn't know the material well, you might fall for this.
- Make a guess on a question that you do not know the answer to. There is no penalty for an incorrect answer. Eliminate the answer choices that you know are incorrect. For example, this will let your guess be a 1 in 3 chance instead.

 Legal Note

All rights reserved. This Study Guide, Book and Flashcards are protected under US Copyright Law. No part of this book or study guide or flashcards may be reproduced, distributed or stored in a retrieval system, or transmitted in any form or by any means, electronic, mechanical, photocopying, recording, or otherwise, without the prior written permission of the publisher Breely Crush Publishing, LLC. DSST is a registered trademark of The Thomson Corporation and its affiliated companies, and does not endorse this book.

FLASHCARDS

This section contains flashcards for you to use to further your understanding of the material and test yourself on important concepts, names or dates. Read the term or question then flip the page over to check the answer on the back. Keep in mind that this information may not be covered in the text of the study guide. Take your time to study the flashcards, you will need to know and understand these concepts to pass the test.

The Principles of Scientific Management	Hawthorne Effect
Theory X	Locus of Control
Hierarchy of Needs	Lowest Level Need
ERG	The need for achievement was developed by

When an interest in people changes the effect on the output	Frederick Taylor
Julian Rotter	When people dislike work and responsibility
Physical needs, food, water, shelter	Maslow's
David McClelland	Existence needs, relatedness needs and growth needs

Four Stages of Groups

Trait Theories

Autocratic Leadership

Democratic Leadership

Laissez-faire Leadership

What model is used in decision making?

Body Language

Charisma

Focused on background and personality	Forming, Storming, Norming, Conforming
When the leader uses group ideas and input to make decisions	When the leader keeps the power and makes decisions alone
Vroom and Yetton	When a leader gives a group total control to make decision
Leadership characteristics that inspire employees is called	The way that people communicate with each other using their bodies

Functional	Line and Staff
Matrix	Implicit Favorite Model
When you are selecting a new location for a second office, this decision would be considered	Bounded Rationality Model
Believed that managers make decisions based on their assumptions of human nature	When someone is producing at standard it is called

The organizational structure where there are staff departments support other departments	The organizational structure where a group performing a specialized task reports to a manager in that same area
When a manager makes a decision then looks for information to justify the decision, it is called	The organizational structure where organizations are structured around a special project or event
When you find the answer to your problem but settle for something else is an example of the	Nonprogrammed
Norm	McGregor

Information that is difficult to measure is called	Extrinsic Reinforcement
Storming	Cohesiveness
Values	Humanistic
Top Down	Econological Model

Getting a scholarship because of good grades in an example of	Qualitative
How well the group works together is called	Which of the following is the second step when forming a group
Believing that all people are good	Standards or principles
Choosing the solution that has the greatest benefit	When communication is given from the CEO to his subordinates it is called

The three types of resistance	**Theory Y**
Naturalistic Observation	**What are the five basic traits of personality?**
Role Conflicts	**Three reasons people join groups**
Path-goal theory leaders	**Contingency Theory**

Assuming that all people like and enjoy work	Logical, psychological, sociological
Emotional stability extroversion, openness, good nature, preciseness	Observing information in an unobtrusive manner
Social interaction, need for acceptance, self-esteem	When two people have overlapping job functions
The style of leadership should change based on the situation	Make a path to a goal and help clear the obstacles

NOTES

NOTES

NOTES

NOTES

NOTES

NOTES

NOTES

NOTES

NOTES

NOTES

NOTES

NOTES

NOTES

NOTES

NOTES

NOTES

www.ingramcontent.com/pod-product-compliance
Lightning Source LLC
Chambersburg PA
CBHW081833300426
44116CB00014B/2574